"Monsignor Toups's rector's conferences reflect a deep personal love of the priesthood and an inspired ability to share that love with future priests. Spiritually and theologically rich, his counsels to seminarians flow from a pastoral sensitivity nourished by priestly fraternity, parish experience, and keen insights into what today's Church expects of its future leaders. (A good checklist for those of us already ordained as well!)"

Cardinal Edwin O'Brien
Grand Master of the Order of the Holy Sepulchre

"Drawing upon years of experience in vocations ministry, seminary formation, and administration, Toups seamlessly weaves the spiritual, pastoral, human, and intellectual dimensions of formation into an engaging series of essays that will affirm and challenge seminarians and faculty alike. *The Priests We Need* is a formational gem to be learned from and prayed with by every seminarian and formator."

Father John Kartje
Rector
Mundelein Seminary, Mundelein, Illinois

"Monsignor Toups distills the fruit of his prayer and his extensive experience forming men for parish ministry into a book that treats thorny formation topics in a positive and practical way. This book will be a source of encouragement and wisdom for many seminarians—and for those of us who strive to form them!"

Father Carter Griffin
Vice-Rector
Saint John Paul II Seminary, Washington, DC

"I highly recommend this book because of its practicality, reflection on the four dimensions of priestly formation, and its usefulness in identifying opportunities for men to be formed for priesthood after the mind of Christ. Reading this book will assist in making seminarians ready to serve the Church during challenging times. This resource is a rich resource for all levels of priestly formation."

Sister Marysia Weber, RSM, DO
Saint Louis Archdiocesan Review Board, St Louis, Missouri

The Priests We Need
A Rector Speaks to His Seminarians

Monsignor David L. Toups

The Institute for Priestly Formation
IPF Publications

NIHIL OBSTAT: Father Matthew J. Gutowski, JCL

IMPRIMATUR: Most Reverend George J. Lucas
                Archbishop of Omaha, Nebraska
                July 23, 2019

THE INSTITUTE FOR PRIESTLY FORMATION
IPF Publications
2500 California Plaza
Omaha, Nebraska 68178-0415
www.IPFPublications.com

Printed in the United States of America
ISBN-13: 978-0-9981164-8-8

Cover design by Timothy D. Boatright
Vistra Communications
Tampa, Florida

THE INSTITUTE FOR PRIESTLY FORMATION
Mission Statement

The Institute for Priestly Formation was founded to assist bishops in the spiritual formation of diocesan seminarians and priests in the Roman Catholic Church. The Institute responds to the need to foster spiritual formation as the integrating and governing principle of all aspects for priestly formation. Inspired by the biblical-evangelical spirituality of Ignatius Loyola, this spiritual formation has as its goal the cultivation of a deep interior communion with Christ; from such communion, the priest shares in Christ's own pastoral charity. In carrying out its mission, the Institute directly serves diocesan seminarians and priests as well as those who are responsible for diocesan priestly formation.

THE INSTITUTE FOR PRIESTLY FORMATION
Creighton University
2500 California Plaza
Omaha, Nebraska 68178-0415
www.priestlyformation.org
ipf@creighton.edu

In gratitude to my three rectors who taught by word and example how to be a spiritual father:

Father Thomas O'Dwyer
Edwin Cardinal O'Brien
Timothy Cardinal Dolan

TABLE OF CONTENTS

FOREWORD

At this time a century-or-so ago, a wise Cistercian monk, Jean-Baptiste Chautard, wrote a piece to become a classic of the spiritual life, *The Soul of the Apostolate*. I have treasured its counsel so much that I read it again every Lent. His goal was to urge all of us, especially priests, to make sure that our ministry, our apostolate, our active service to God's people is grounded in and flows from a deep, abiding interior life. He cherished quoting St. Bernard, "Be a reservoir before becoming a channel!" If we needed any further prodding, Chautard offered this spiritual syllogism:

> If the priest is a saint, his people will be fervent; if the pastor is fervent, his parishioners will be pious; if the priest is only pious, the people will at least be decent. But, beware! If the priest is just decent, his people will be godless. The spiritual generation is always one degree less intense in its life than those who beget it in Christ.

"Those who beget it in Christ" are our priests. Thus are priests called to be saints, the most effective service they can render their people.

To summon men to follow the mandate of Jesus, "Cast out to the deep!" (Lk 5:4), is the mission statement of every seminary. The formation of future priests starts with the call, grace, and mercy of Jesus. It is nurtured in the family—often called the "first seminary"—developed in a parish with a school or solid catechetical program, promoted by the example of priests and faithful, fed by the sacraments, inflamed by prayer and service to others. But the intense, official formation of future priests is entrusted to the seminary, where the program shepherded by the rector and faculty is propelled by the encouragement of happy and holy pastors.

If you are looking for an example of how this shepherding can be done well, keep reading this attractive and enlightening book. Monsignor David Toups has been at the acclaimed St. Vincent de Paul Seminary in Florida for over a decade and is now admired for his leadership in the art of preparation for the Sacrament of Holy Orders.

Since *Pastores Dabo Vobis*, the apostolic exhortation of Pope St. John Paul II in 1992, regular *rector's conferences*—where the rector addresses his men on the basics of spiritual, human, theological, and pastoral formation—have become a *sine qua non* of any seminary program.

This book contains samples of Monsignor Toups's conferences. He tells us he speaks as a "spiritual father" to his sons, and that he does indeed. Savor wise counsel and instruction on topics such as hope, building a Catholic culture, freedom as taught by God's Word, and the boost of a Holy Hour. Pay special attention to his *caveats*, such as alcohol abuse, laxity in chastity, a "self-referential" priesthood, an opulent way of life, and the peril of isolationism.

In these days, when we weary of hearing only about scandals by priests, we often ask, "Did not these men hear of these dangers, and were not they warned about them in the seminary?" The candidates Monsignor Toups speaks to certainly are, as is so evident in these conferences. And those of us already configured to Jesus, Head and Shepherd of the Church, can continue on the road to conversion of heart as we branches daily respond to the invitation of the vine, to remain united to Him.

Our people say to us, as did the Greeks to the Apostles, "We want to see Jesus." Well, *Nemo dat quod non habit!* We cannot give Him if we have not got Him! That is the advice of Monsignor Toups to his seminarians.

Timothy Cardinal Dolan
†Archbishop of New York
Feast of St. John Vianney, 2019

INTRODUCTION

In the wake of our most recent outbreak of scandals in the Catholic Church, our seminarians and our faithful need to know that Jesus Christ is still the center of our faith and that the majority of our priests are serving heroically and selflessly in our Church. I have been the rector of a major seminary for over seven years and spent thirteen years total in seminary and formation work. This book of "rector's conferences" is representative of the formation seminarians are receiving across our nation. Every month, rectors speak to the hearts of their seminarians to inspire, encourage, and challenge them to be the best men—men of communion, sacrifice, and prayer—they can be for the sake of the flock entrusted to their care.

These days, the priesthood and our Church are being battered from all sides—and in some instances, rightly so; however, we must not hang our heads in shame as Catholics. In acknowledging the sins and crimes of the past, we must also keep moving forward to proclaim the Gospel message of freedom, light, and joy in the Holy Spirit. We need to be proud of who Christ has called us to be and serve fearlessly in the midst of confusion and chaos. When I spoke to our graduates this year as they departed and prepared for ordination in their respective dioceses, I told them that there has never been a better time to be a priest. We must believe this and know that Jesus has called each of us "for a time like this" (Esther 4:14), to be the agents of change and hope for our Church.

The intention of this short collection of conferences is to inspire and edify those called to the priesthood and those who love the Body of Christ, which is called to be "a light to the nations." Pope Francis has encouraged our priests to "smell like the sheep" and go out to the "existential peripheries" of our society. These are *the priests we need* to serve us for the decades to come. In these pages, you will read about the hope, transparency, integration, freedom, spirituality, and selflessness necessary for a man who is called to the very real and demanding life of priesthood. Only such men of integration, prayer, and humble service will be able to face the challenges of today as chaste-celibate spiritual fathers. Christ must be our "all and in all" (Col 3:11), and He must remain the center of our lives here and for all eternity. Jesus Christ is our model of priesthood, love, and healing; only He can make us whole in this challenging era. Do not give up hope; do not despair for "Jesus Christ is Lord!" (Phil 2:11). May Mary, Mother of Priests, intercede for our Church and form many holy priestly hearts as she formed the Heart of her Son in the home of Nazareth.

Msgr. David L. Toups, STD
Rector/President of St. Vincent de Paul Regional Seminary,
Boynton Beach, Florida
June 28, 2019
Feast of the Most Sacred Heart of Jesus and World Day of Prayer
for the Sanctification of Priests

Seeds of Hope Spread through the Public Witness of the Priest

We hear a lot about "hope and change," but *that* "hope and change" cannot save souls. You, my dear brothers, are the hope that can change the course of human history, thus the title of tonight's conference: "Seeds of Hope Spread through the Public Witness of the Priest."

A little over six years ago, my dear father died after a very short battle with pancreatic cancer. My dad was a man of deep faith, and he faced the end of his life with the courage and conviction of a Christian. He took as his motto that of Padre Pio: "Pray, hope, and don't worry." Is that not exactly what each of us should be doing on a daily basis? As St. Paul wrote to the Romans: "Rejoice in hope, endure in affliction, persevere in prayer" (Rm 12:12). Rejoice in hope, and persevere in prayer! The Christian always lives with hope. My dad knew his citizenship was in heaven and that, no matter what, as he walked his daily journey not knowing precisely when his impending death would come, for him, life was Christ and death was victory.[1]

Hope is the theological virtue that keeps us looking "forward to the resurrection of the dead and the life of the world to come."[2] Hope reminds us we are never alone and that, no matter how dark the hour may seem, we are never abandoned. When Pope Benedict XVI came for his apostolic visit to the United States in 2006, he chose as his theme: "Christ our Hope!" In 2007, he also chose the topic of hope for his second encyclical letter entitled *Spe Salvi*. Pope Benedict XVI wrote:

> When no one listens to me anymore, God still listens to me. When I can no longer talk to anyone or call upon anyone, I can always talk to God. When there is no longer anyone to help me deal with a need or expectation that goes beyond the human capacity for hope, he can help me. When I have been plunged into complete solitude . . . ; if I pray I am never totally alone. The late Cardinal Nguyen Van Thuan, a prisoner for thirteen years, nine of them spent in solitary confinement, has left us a precious little book: *Prayers of Hope*. During thirteen years in jail, in a situation of seemingly utter hopelessness, the fact that he could listen and speak to God became for him an increasing power of hope, which enabled him, after his release, to become for people all over the world a witness to hope—to that great hope which does not wane even in the nights of solitude.[3]

Hope is the fundamental virtue that keeps us focused on the positive in the midst of seeming defeat. "Where, O death, is your victory? Where, O death, is your sting?" (1 Cor 15:55). That is why we pray daily in the Embolism of the Lord's Prayer: "as we await the blessed hope and the coming of our Savior, Jesus Christ!" *Beatam spem*—blessed hope! We have one Savior, and He will deliver us! The questions we must regularly ask ourselves are: Am I living for heaven? Is my life focused on the final goal every day?

On the pinnacle of the Basilica of St. Paul's in Rome is a beautiful marble cross with the words "*spes unica*" inserted in mosaic. The Cross is our only hope. Think of the image of the Great Cross in St. Augustine on the seminary's Year of Faith prayer card. The Mystery of the Cross—Christ's Passion, Death, and Resurrection—is truly our only hope. Without Christ, life is hopeless! That is why our task of priestly formation is so urgent: the world needs you to offer hope. A priestly life well lived offers just such hope to the world. We must know who we are and be firmly grounded in the faith to offer hope to our brothers and sisters. That is why the author of Hebrews writes, "Be strongly encouraged to hold fast to the hope that lies before us. This we have as an anchor of the soul, sure and firm" (Heb 6:18–19). Hope anchors us and keeps us firmly moored during the storms of life. In the face of sickness and death, in the face of loneliness and frustration, in the face of sorrow and distress, hope helps us to overcome because Christ is our hope!

We have spoken about our need to be credible witnesses; and today, we speak of our need to be hope-filled witnesses. Our Holy Father wrote, "Hope in a Christian sense is always hope for others as well. It is an active hope, in which we struggle to prevent things moving towards the 'perverse end.' It is an active hope also in the sense that we keep the world open to God. Only in this way does it continue to be a truly human hope."[4] Hope is not individualistic; it is always open to others and is for others.[5] We are to be seeds of hope in the midst of our Church and society.

I now want to take a more practical look at four ways in which we bring hope into the world and then conversely, the pitfalls that can cause despair.

Represent a High Standard

The faithful want to see something different in us. As St. Paul wrote, "Do not conform yourselves to this age but be transformed by the renewal of your mind, that you may discern what is the will of God, what is good and pleasing and perfect" (Rom 12:2). Be transformed by your time in priestly formation, transformed more and more into the image and likeness of Christ Himself. Remember, the word for "holy" in Hebrew is *kadosh*, meaning separated. We are called daily to enter into the Holy of Holies in order to be transformed. "Prayer is the school of hope," according to Pope Benedict XVI.[6] As priests and future priests, we are to foster a "monasticism of the heart," an inner sanctum in which we encounter the living God and allow Him to form us on a daily basis.[7] When we are in the parish or even on vacation, our schedules and daily horarium should look different from those of other people our age—Does my life revolve around God? Is it marked by times of prayer? Am I in relationship and seeking communion with the Blessed Trinity? The heart open to this kind of ongoing conversion offers great hope to the world. When people see we are striving for holiness, we bring them great hope!

The reverse side of this coin is when we try to be like everyone else. Parishioners really do want more from us. Whether it is our use of language, perceived inappropriate relationships, the way we dress, our use of alcohol, our social activities, or any form of a worldly lifestyle, the simple fact is that the priest is always and necessarily under scrutiny. The *Code of Canon Law* reminds us, "Clerics are to follow a simple way of life and avoid anything which smacks of worldliness

(*vanitatem*)."[8] Regarding our call not to be conformed to
this age, I would like to say a few words about the use of
alcohol and invite us to pay close attention to any abuse of
this substance and its addictive nature. A priest who drinks
heavily does not engender hope in the people of God. We
heard St. Paul's admonition in Monday's Liturgy that leaders
not be drunkards (Ti 1:8–9). This insidious vice can sneak up
and bite us if we are not cautious, prudent, and moderate in
our drinking. The *Catechism of the Catholic Church* reminds us
that "the virtue of temperance disposes us to *avoid every kind
of excess*: the abuse of food, alcohol, tobacco, or medicine."[9]
There is *never* a reason to have more than two to three drinks
as a maximum. I pray this is not an issue in our house of
formation, but I have heard of occasional abuses in the past.
Such abuse will be addressed in the future out of love and
concern for the individual and the people of God.

Be Present and Available

When needed, be present for the joys and sorrows of
people's lives, especially the sorrows—we offer hope for eternal life and remind the faithful that God has not abandoned
them. I think back to moments I have spent with the dying
or ministering to families in the intensive care unit. What
might not seem like a big deal or what might have seemed
like an inconvenience can be life changing for the person in
need. The stories I still hear from my first assignment fifteen
years ago humble me because very often, I simply do not
remember these pivotal moments parishioners experienced.
Being a good priest is not rocket science. It is as easy as "just
showing up"; the self-oblation and availability we offer make
all the difference in the world. Being present in order to bring

hope can happen when we are not even trying. A priest who is in the regular habit of wearing the Roman collar will be a billboard for eternity as he goes about his daily business. Do not underestimate the power of our priestly presence in the marketplace—indeed, we offer hope!

On the flip side, when we do not show up when we are needed or when we fail to return calls from parishioners in a timely fashion, we fail to offer them hope. The priests in my former parish, Christ the King, could be counted on; and people deeply appreciated it. There were times the answering service would call us when they could not reach the neighboring parish. Now, mind you, it made me crazy when other churches would show a lack of responsibility by not answering their emergency line—I would later contact the pastor to find out if there was an issue as to why their call needed to be answered by us. But the point is there were souls who needed a priest, and our pastoral zeal to help must override our personal comfort. Despair and distress (and a few nasty phone calls) follow when we do not respond to our people in need. God will use you on countless occasions as an instrument of healing and hope for His people.

Another important moment to be present is on Sundays. This may sound obvious, but you might be surprised to find the day that should have "all hands on deck" is not always so. When we do not show up on Sundays to greet and assist with Holy Communion, we are missing a huge opportunity to be present to our family. The faithful will never get to know, love, and trust us if they only see us at the Masses we celebrate in our monthly rotation. The little things matter—you bring hope when you just show up at Mass, at meetings, at the hospital, at the Knights of Columbus fish fry, at school, or even at the occasional First Communion party.

Prioritize Parish Youth

Make the youth in your parish a priority—they are the hope for the future of the Church. Occasionally, I hear of a newly-ordained priest telling the pastor, "I don't do youth ministry"—wrong answer. We do whatever our parish needs. I remember showing up to my first assignment and being told by the pastor to get on a bus the next day to drive up to Atlanta with one hundred teens I had never met before. That was frightening, but the fruit of a priestly presence makes all the difference in the world when it comes to young people. The bonds I made with the youth on that trip resulted in weddings, baptisms, seminarians, and a religious sister. Teens and college-age students are like sponges desiring to soak up the Truth. If we shun our responsibility as spiritual fathers, then we will lose the battle of transforming our society. Our youth need us to bring them hope, and their youthful zeal and unjaded innocence offer us hope in return.

When we show no interest in the New Evangelization and the New Generation of young people, we cannot be surprised when they flock to the evangelical Church down the street. A former parishioner came up to me when I first arrived and said that his daughters were all going to an evangelical youth group and that he would have very much preferred them to be exposed to the riches of our Catholic faith. My first hire was a director of youth ministry; and two years later, his daughters, who were beginning to drift from the Church, became leaders among our own youth group. We offer hope to the whole parish when they see an active and vibrant youth ministry. Funds and human resources must be allocated to make it happen, and the active presence of one of the parish priests is paramount for its success. As the newly ordained, that will most likely fall to you—get ready!

Preach on Difficult Issues

Preach on difficult issues, but only after the faithful get to know you and know that you have their best interests in mind. After you have established spiritual clout, they will follow you, their shepherd. Now, I do not mean preaching a fire and brimstone homily every week, but there are appropriate occasions throughout the year in which we must speak the Truth of the Church's teaching. We now live in a nation where the majority no longer holds to traditional Judeo-Christian values. It has recently become quite evident that the moral teachings of the Church are no longer valued by mainstream society nor, sadly, by many Catholics as well, whether on the nature of and the indissolubility of marriage between a man and a woman, contraception, abortion, euthanasia, fetal stem cell research, religious liberty, and so on. You give hope to the faithful that the Church still has a moral voice when you preach the Truth in Love. Our vocation reminds our parishioners that we are all "here to get out of here"—to live in freedom, draw closer to the Lord, and get to heaven, where our true citizenship lies.

When the faithful do not hear the Good News preached, they get discouraged. Words of encouragement, counsel, and even—at times—words of challenge offered in love and with the Gospel message of Christ as the center bring our people great hope. When we fail to live and preach prophetically, we offer the faithful no hope for the future. Our ministry is not social work; we must not cease striving to "save souls" and build up the Kingdom. We have the opportunity to bring great joy and hope or be the source of despair and distrust. *Gaudium et spes* are the first words of the Vatican II document on the Church in the modern world. *Gaudium et spes*: joy and hope. If we are to make Christ and His Church relevant in today's world, we must be men of joy and hope. We bring hope to the faithful by being fully integrated men—certainly human, certainly men who make mistakes—but men who are striving to be men of faith, not drawing attention to ourselves but to Christ. We are "earthen vessels" (2 Cor 4:7), recognizing that from the beginning, Christ called a bunch of characters. *We* are comforted and given *hope* by the words of our Lord: "It was not you who chose me, but I who chose you and appointed you to go and bear fruit" (Jn 15:16).

Due to scandal in the Church, many have had their faith shaken regarding the very nature of the priesthood. While the Sacraments are not dependent upon the worthiness of the minister, priests have a responsibility, as ordained, to respond to the gift received at ordination. For the sake of God's people, priests must foster their personal character and align it with the sacramental character received at ordination so they may be credible witnesses in order that the world may believe in Him who sent us.[10] Father Federico Suarez writes, "Each individual must behave in accordance with what he is. The priest, a consecrated man, has a special quality, the quality of something holy, for his sacramental consecration endows him with a sacred character. He can no longer behave as if this special quality did not exist. He is a man of God, belonging no longer to himself but to God alone."[11] We are certainly not better than anyone else, but because of our state in life as an ordained witness to Christ, the call to holiness is elevated and the obligation is inherent to be a man of extraordinary virtue.

In today's world, and even in the Church, there is a temptation to despair. However, Christian hope, the theological virtue, must be the rock of our lives. The great French writer Georges Bernanos once wrote about "real hope." He said it "must be won. [We] can only attain hope through truth, at the cost of great effort and long patience. . . . Hope is a virtue, *virtus*, strength; a heroic determination of the soul. [And] the highest form of hope is despair overcome."[12] St. Paul reminds us in Romans 5:3-5 [emphasis added]: "We even boast of our afflictions, knowing that affliction produces endurance, and endurance, proven character, and proven character, *hope*, and *hope* does not disappoint, because the love of God has been poured out into our hearts through the holy Spirit that has been given to us." Remain steadfast; remain in His love; "the highest form of hope is despair overcome."[13] Christ is our hope!

As I close tonight, I want to quote at length from a writing of the late second century called *The Letter to Diognetus*, in which the community is commended to keep their eyes on heaven as their true homeland:

> Christians are indistinguishable from other men either by nationality, language or customs. . . .

> And yet there is something extraordinary about their lives. They live in their own countries as though they were only passing through. They play their full role as citizens, but labor under all the disabilities of aliens. Any country

can be their homeland, but for them their homeland, wherever it may be, is a foreign country. . . .

They live in the flesh, but they are not governed by the desires of the flesh. They pass their days upon earth, but they are citizens of heaven. Obedient to the laws, they yet live on a level that transcends the law. Christians love all men, but all men persecute them. Condemned because they are not understood, they are put to death, but raised to life again. They live in poverty, but enrich many; they are totally destitute, but possess an abundance of everything. They suffer dishonor, but that is their glory. They are defamed, but vindicated. A blessing is their answer to abuse, deference their response to insult. For the good they do they receive the punishment of malefactors, but even then they, rejoice, as though receiving the gift of life. . . .

To speak in general terms, we may say that the Christian is to the world what the soul is to the body. As the soul is present in every part of the body, while remaining distinct from it, so Christians are found in all the cities of the world, but cannot be identified with the world. As the visible body contains the invisible soul, so Christians are seen living in the world, but their religious life remains unseen. The body hates the soul and wars against it, not because of any injury the soul has done it, but because of the restriction the soul places on its pleasures. Similarly, the world hates the Christians, not because they have done it any wrong, but because they are opposed to its enjoyments.

Christians love those who hate them just as the soul loves the body and all its members despite the body's hatred.

It is by the soul, enclosed within the body, that the body is held together, and similarly, it is by the Christians, detained in the world as in a prison, that the world is held together. The soul, though immortal, has a mortal dwelling place; and Christians also live for a time amidst perishable things, while awaiting the freedom from change and decay that will be theirs in heaven. As the soul benefits from the deprivation of food and drink, so Christians flourish under persecution. Such is the Christian's lofty and divinely appointed function, from which he is not permitted to excuse himself.[14]

Now *that* is "hope and change" we can believe in because Christ is our hope! It is said that "hope springs eternal"; indeed, hope moves us forward to eternal life. May our world see this hope proclaimed through our lives.

We now turn to our Blessed Mother in order to be fortified and encouraged, to be reminded that our citizenship is in heaven with her Divine Son, our Lord and Savior, Jesus Christ our King!

Mary, you are our life, our sweetness, and our *hope*.

Pray for us, O holy Mother of God; that we may be made worthy of the promises of Christ.

NOTES

1. See Philippians 1:21-23.
2. *Nicene Creed.*
3. Benedict XVI, *Spe Salvi* (2007), sec. 32.
4. Ibid., sec. 34.
5. See *Spe Salvi*, sec. 28.
6. Ibid., sec. 32.
7. George A. Aschenbrenner, S.J., *Quickening the Fire in Our Midst* (Chicago: Loyola Press, 2002).
8. Code of Canon Law: Latin-English Edition: New English Translation (Codex Iuris Canonici [CIC]), (Washington, DC: Canon Law Society of America, 1998), c. 282.
9. *Catechism of the Catholic Church* (Washington, DC: USCCB Publishing, 2000), sec. 2290. Emphasis in original.
10. See John 17:21.
11. Federico Suarez, *About Being a Priest* (Princeton, NJ: Scepter Press, 1996), 11.
12. Georges Bernanos, *The Heroic Face of Innocence: Three Stories by Georges Bernanos*, chapter entitled "Sermon of an Agnostic on the Feast of St. Therese," (Grand Rapids, MI: Eerdmans Publishing, [original 1938] 1999 edition), 26.
13. Ibid.
14. From a letter to Diognetus (Nn. 5-6; Funk, 397-401) as found on www.vatican.va/spirit/documents/spirit_20010522_diogneto_en.html (accessed 5/6/19).

Anima Christi

I recently ran across an inspiring talk by Archbishop Jorge Carlos Patrón Wong of the Congregation for the Clergy who is in charge of seminary formation and the implementation of the new *Ratio Fundamentalis*[1]:

> An important element in accompaniment is *trust* (Cfr. RFIS, 47), with which the candidate is able to entrust his life to another person, handing over his own intimacy. *Respect*, *empathy*, *listening*, are, among others, the keys to help the seminarian grow in trust within an interpersonal relationship. When one feels heard one learns to entrust one's life to another. One is only willing to embrace a piece of advice or a proposal when one feels listened to, before that it is difficult to do so. We need, as companions, to learn how to listen, and to listen not only to what is communicated verbally but, especially, to what is expressed in non-verbal ways, which constitute the greater part of the communication.[2]

This quote has served as a good reminder to me, as spiritual father and rector, and I hope also to you, that both sides of our house—faculty and seminarians—are to remain in trusting and open dialogue. I am so grateful for my listening sessions with the first and second theologians, the pre-theologians, and numerous others with whom I have met in order to hear your comments and consider your recommendations. As you know, I have always had an open-door policy when you have cares and concerns you would like to bring to me. These meetings have been a real grace for me as you shared your gratitude for our professors and their contributions to your formation. We really do care and love each of you on this journey and want to foster your vocation and give you the very best formation we can, although sometimes that love comes through like a fire hydrant instead of a water fountain! At the end of tonight's conference, I will share some of the ideas the seminary staff is discerning for next year.

First, let us look at our integrating relationship with Christ, from which all else flows. We can make all kinds of changes—and if you ask the older brothers in the house, they can tell you we do so regularly—but if we do not root all in Christ, we are just spinning our wheels. Archbishop Patrón Wong refers to the need for our interiorization of what he calls a "mystical identification with the person of Jesus."[3] As you deepen your relationship with Christ during these years of the Discipleship and Configuration Stages, you will begin to relate to St. Paul who writes: "I have been crucified with Christ; yet I live, no longer I, but Christ lives in me" (Gal 2:19b–20). That is the real purpose of all formation—both initially while in the seminary and ongoing after ordination—to allow Christ to live in and through us. This is not just something we can "do," but rather, we must "allow" Jesus to be configured within us. *You* must allow it since *you* are the main "protagonist" of your own formation.[4] *Christ* is the point of integration! In fact, the *Ratio* envisions that each of the four dimensions[5] leads us into greater configuration with Him:

> Each of the dimensions of formation is aimed at "transforming" or "assimilating" the heart in the image of the heart of Christ, who was sent by the Father to fulfil [*sic*] his loving plan. . . . As the Second Vatican Council indicates, the entire process of formation in preparation for priestly ministry, in fact, has as its aim the preparation of seminarians to "*enter into communion with the charity of Christ the Good Shepherd.*"[6]

As I reflected and prayed on each of the dimensions and our call to mystically identify with Christ, the *Anima Christi*, arose with me. As we now pray this prayer, let us invite Christ to dwell within our souls, bodies, minds, and hearts.

> *Soul of Christ, sanctify me.*
> *Body of Christ, save me.*
> *Blood of Christ, inebriate me.*
> *Water from the side of Christ, wash me.*
> *Passion of Christ, strengthen me.*
> *O Good Jesus, hear me.*
> *Within your wounds conceal me.*
> *Do not permit me to be parted from you.*
> *From the evil foe, protect me.*
> *At the hour of my death call me.*
> *And bid me come to you,*
> *to praise you with all your saints*
> *for ever and ever.*
> *Amen.*

How do I live an integrated human formation? By taking on the "Body of Christ." Christ dwells within us, and we need

to be conscious of the fact that everything we say and do is
to be in union with Him who dwells within us! Only then
does human formation begin to make sense. Our bodies are
given for Him Who gave His body for us and Who continues
to do so every day on the altar. "To that end, the seminarian
is called upon to develop his personality, having Christ, the
perfect man, as his model and source."[7] Human formation
is about much more than the externals, but the outer man is
meant to reflect our inner realities. Christ is our model and
source—"Body of Christ, save me!"

Spiritual formation is integrated into our mystical identification and configuration in the "Soul of Christ," Christ's
soul dwelling within us. "The heart of spiritual formation is
personal union with Christ, which is born of, and nourished
in, a particular way by prolonged and silent prayer."[8] Our
daily prayer and dialogue with the Father is done in union
with Christ. The words of St. Augustine come to mind: "He
prays for us as our priest, he prays in us as our head, he is
the object of our prayers as our God. . . . We pray then to
him, through him, in him, and we speak along with him
and he along with us."[9] Being ever more conscious of this
truth, we can unite our souls to His and say, "Soul of Christ,
sanctify me!"

Intellectual formation finds its source of integration in
the "mind of Christ" (1 Cor 2:16). As we study and take in
the Word-Made-Flesh, we are also united to Him, allowing
Christ to form our thoughts; and we absorb His teaching in a
spirit of humility and docility to the Truth. This "forming of
the mind" comes about through a transformation and con-
formation of the mind of Christ.[10] According to St. Paul, we
are called to have the "mind of Christ" (1 Cor 2:16). When

we study, read, and write, we do so "in Christ" and for His holy people. The rigors of study only really make sense in this context. Even when we feel overwhelmed, we invite Christ into the given moment to help us discern what we can actually do with the time entrusted to us.

We are encouraged in intellectual formation to grow in sacrifice, diligence, and character. The seminary staff certainly wants you to fall in love with theology and have a more integrated culture of learning in the seminary that will remain with you throughout priesthood. At the same time, we all recognize there is hard work involved in this endeavor, particularly in one's seminary years. Integration occurs in the mind of Christ "who learned obedience from what he suffered" (Heb 5:8). Put on the mind of Christ—"O Blood of Christ, inebriate me!"

Of course, pastoral formation is integrated when we unite our hearts with the "Heart of Christ," the Good Shepherd. According to the *Ratio*, "The gaze of the Good Shepherd, who seeks out, walks alongside and leads his sheep, will form a serene, prudent and compassionate outlook in [the seminarian]."[11] Our pastoral charity and love expressed in ministry is precisely what allows Christ to love through us. We cannot love like Christ if we do not allow Him to do it through us. Trust that God wants to give us precisely such a heart, which allows us to be a greater self-gift to others. In fact, it is only in the crucified and risen Christ that the path of integration finds meaning and completion; all things are united in Him,[12] so that *"God may be all in all."*[13] "Passion of Christ, strengthen me!"

Affective maturity in the seminarian means he can give himself without reserve to these four dimensions of formation by inserting himself into Christ. Integration happens when we are present to God in prayer, which allows us to be present to the people of God in our daily lives. The quality of the presence we give to God will be the quality of the presence we give to the people. Be with Him; dwell in Him; allow Him to dwell in you. As our Lord tells us in the fifteenth chapter of St. John's Gospel: "Remain in me, as I remain in you. Just as a branch cannot bear fruit on its own unless it remains on the vine, so neither can you unless you remain in me" (Jn 15:4). This "remaining in" is the source of our mystical identification in Christ as well as the source of our identity, our pastoral authority, and our zeal and fire of love for souls. We are to strive to be "configured to Christ, Head and Shepherd, Servant and Spouse. . . . These characteristics of the person of Christ help us to understand better the ministerial priesthood in the Church."[14]

Relationship. Identity. Mission. By learning to relate all to Jesus and allowing Him to dwell in our bodies, souls, minds, and hearts, we grow in our identity of being configured to Him. Then, the undertaking of missionary discipleship, the passion and zeal of our pastoral hearts, will flow unreservedly and freely from and through us.

Let us turn back to listening. To allow the depth and breadth of study and prayer needed in your lives, the seminary staff is listening to your input and studying the horarium. We so desire to make space for you so that you can live in the seminary with a less "frenetic pace" and your hearts can be formed in contemplative prayer and study, allowing the four dimensions to "interact simultaneously. . . . Each of the dimensions of formation is aimed at 'transforming' or 'assimilating' the heart in the image of the heart of Christ."[15]

This puts pressure on us to help provide for you; and it puts pressure on you to be responsible for what is given to you—we are called to be good stewards entrusting all to Christ. This means conversion for us all! What are some things you have brought forward?

- Desiring a more consistent daily schedule

- Wanting better blocks of time for consecrated and dedicated study

  - I found the brief video synopsis of Cal Newport's book *Deep Work: Rules for Focused Success in a Distracted World* to be insightful.[16]

  - Tonight, I am giving you a wonderful booklet entitled *Wonder and the Prayerful Study of Theology.*[17]

- Preferring more collaboration and communication among the faculty teaching in each year of the program, to ensure a balanced study and workload

- Fostering greater awareness among the faculty of those studying in a second language

Of course, we are unable to alter some things in a seminary schedule, but we have always done our best to listen and make necessary adjustments as needs arise. Although some of you may not be aware of it, the faculty and administration continually collaborate with the student council; certainly, ask upperclassmen or look at past student council minutes, and you will see many changes have been made that were brought forward through your initiatives. As faculty and seminarians, let us work hard as a community of faith to reject the evil one who scatters and divides (*diabolein*) and instead, build a hermeneutic of trust, gratitude, and integration. Let us be united in our mission in the Heart of Christ, our integrating principle. This is a good time for us to pray again the second half of the *Anima Christi*:

> *O Good Jesus, hear me.*
> *Within your wounds conceal me.*
> *Do not permit me to be parted from you.*
> *From the evil foe protect me.*
> *At the hour of my death call me.*
> *And bid me come to you,*
> *To praise you with all your saints*
> *for ever and ever.*
> *Amen.*

Brothers, we do not want you to be workaholics, which leads to isolation and does not nurture relationship with God or others. Rather, we want you to be hard workers who remain in communion with Christ at all times: at prayer, study, leisure, apostolate, and so on. This is the true integration and balance the Church needs of us, despite our schedules, because we know that Christ is dwelling within: we have taken on His Body, soul, mind, and heart. At times, this certainly entails self-denial, trust, and obedience to the process of priestly formation; but you are not doing it alone. You are doing it with and for Christ, guided by your daily prayer and spiritual direction. I wish to close with the *Serenity Prayer*, which gives us an apt tone for moving forward as a community of faith: "God grant me the *serenity* to accept the things I cannot change; *courage* to change the things I can; and *wisdom* to know the difference."[18]

NOTES

1.   Congregation for the Clergy, *Ratio Fundamentalis Institutionis Sacerdotalis* (Vatican City: L'Osservatore Romano, 2016).

2.   Jorge Carlos Patrón Wong, "Fundamental Principles of the New RFIS: Singular Journey of Discipleship, Integral, Communitarian, Missionary," (2017), 7. Emphasis in original. http://www.clerus.va/content/dam/clerus/Dox/Fundamental%20Principles%20of%20the%20New%20RFIS.pdf (accessed February 6, 2019).

3.   Jorge Carlos Patrón Wong, "Foundations of Priestly Formation," (n.d.), 5. http://www.clerus.va/content/dam/clerus/Dox/Conference%20-%20Foundations%20of%20Priestly%20Formation.pdf (accessed February 6, 2019).

4.   *Ratio Fundamentalis Institutionis Sacerdotalis*, sec. 130.

5.   See John Paul II, *Pastores Dabo Vobis* (1992), sec. 43-59 for details about the four dimensions of priestly formation: human, spiritual, intellectual, and pastoral.

6.   Ibid., sec. 89.

7.   Ibid., sec. 93.

8.   Ibid., sec. 102.

9.   St. Augustine, "Discourse on Psalm 85," as found in *Liturgy of the Hours*, vol. I (New York: Catholic Book Publishing Co., 1975), 26.

10.   See *Ratio Fundamentalis*, sec. 118.

11.   Ibid., sec. 120.

12.   See Ephesians 1:10

13.   See 1 Corinthians 15:28. Emphasis added.

14.   Ibid., sec. 35.

15.   Ibid., sec. 89.

16.   Brian Johnson, "PNTV: Deep Work by Cal Newport," *YouTube* video, 20:26 (Oct . 27, 2015), synopsis of *Deep Work: Rules for Focused Success in a Distracted World* by Cal Newport (New York: Grand Central Publishing, 2016). https://youtu.be/KX_2a_jsGYw (accessed February 6, 2019).

17.   John Gresham and Thomas Neal, *Wonder and the Prayerful Study of Theology: A Meditation for Seminarians* (Omaha, NE: Institute for Priestly Formation, 2017).

18.   This quote is often attributed to Reinhold Neibuhr.

Catholic Cultural Awareness

We live in an era of ever heightened racial and social tension. If you turn on the nightly news, you will hear about Black Lives Matter, Islamophobia, heated immigration debates, protests, police shootings, and terrorism—both foreign and domestic—in the name of religion. These realities point out that deep racial and ethnic tension still exists in our culture here in the United States. As priests, we need to bring some sense and healing to the current state of affairs. We would be naïve to believe our own vision is not tainted by the realities we see in the twenty-four-hour news cycle; so tonight, let us look more deeply at what it means to be Catholic, how to be more aware of others, and how to value each other's cultural differences. Being healers in the midst of division is nothing new and goes all the way back to the earliest of Church experiences. In Acts 6:1, the Hellenists complained against those of Jewish descent that their widows were being neglected. Do not despair, the challenges of our time are no less unsurmountable than they were in the year 33 or 1965—God gives each of us the grace to minister in our present age.

One of the most memorable images from World Youth Day Krakow was when, welcoming the Holy Father to the

Vigil, we looked out and saw the waving flags representing the nationalities of the 2.8 million young people in attendance. In particular, there was a grouping of countries that would normally never be seen together: Israel, Lebanon, Syria, and Iraq. To see these young people of warring nations in the same sector and joined in communion was awe inspiring and hopeful for the future of their people. It is their belief that something much larger unites them. It is not their nationality; it is their belief in God and our common humanity. In a word, it is because they are Catholic! Is this not what unites us?

What does it mean to be Catholic? Does it mean more than correctly celebrating the Liturgy or hanging a picture of the Pope in every classroom? Of course, we do these things; and, of course, being Catholic is about a whole lot more than these things. We know the etymology of the word comes from two Greek words, *kata* and *holos*, meaning "according to the whole," or more colloquially, "universal." Being Catholic is about recognizing we belong to the whole and, in some ways, the whole belongs to us. We belong to something so much greater than ourselves, than our parish, than our seminary, than our Church in the United States. We belong to the one, Holy, Catholic, and apostolic Church. St. Augustine reminds us in the Office of Readings that "our Mother, the Catholic Church has given birth to all faithful Christians scattered over the whole world."[1] This reality should stretch our horizon of national boundaries and regional disputes to help us realize we belong to the whole and are called to pray for and care for the whole. We are meant to influence the world through our catholicity.

The multicultural face of our Church in the United States is a tremendous blessing of vitality and enrichment. Today, just over one-third of the Catholic population in the United States is Hispanic or Latino,[2] and another 8 percent are African American, Asian, Native American, or Pacific Islander.[3] About 26 percent—one in four churches across the United States—of all parishes specifically serve Latino communities,[4] and the proportion is obviously higher in Florida. The Center for Applied Research in the Apostolate's[5] "The CARA Report" is always a good source of trend data, and I encourage you to become familiar with their work.

We do not have to look too far to realize the extraordinary reality of diversity in our Church. We do not have to go to World Youth Day or be at a Wednesday audience in St. Peter's Square; we just have to open our eyes in the present moment. Look around at each other: our students, faculty, and staff at St. Vincent de Paul (SVDP) Regional Seminary represent over twenty-five countries of origin—that is amazing. We have a truly "Catholic" treasure in our midst. Every year, there is a question on your end-of-the-year evaluation related to "global awareness"—become more conscious of this lived reality in our midst.

SVDP Regional Seminary is a bilingual and multicultural institution. Have we integrated this statement into a lived reality? Have we really appreciated what a gift it is to be able to learn from and share in such a diversity of cultures? Have we failed to recognize the opportunity to value the incredible beauty of different cultures? Can we see the myriad ways people have come to live and be in this world, reflecting the image and likeness of God? We all bring perspectives from our past and from societal views; but here, we are presented with this amazing opportunity to learn and love and expand our horizons. It is not enough, then, just to tolerate each other; we must truly strive to value and appreciate each other. I ask these questions today because I think we sometimes allow the baggage of our past or our biases to skew our present perception of reality. How can we grow in sensitivity and awareness of the other who is our brother or sister, not just for the sake of running our house, but most importantly, so we can be priests who minister to the needs of all with a cultural awareness and sensitivity that is truly Catholic?

Pope Francis recently reminded priests: "With the oil of hope and consolation, he [the priest] becomes neighbor to each person, careful to share in their abandonment and suffering. Having given up self-determination, he has no agenda to protect, but each morning consigns his time to meet the Lord so as to be free to meet and be approached by people."[6] If we are to be effective priests, we must pray to have vision that sees the value and dignity of each race, culture, and country of origin; otherwise, biases that may have been engrained in us from our youth may cloud our vision. This is more than just being "color blind" but having the eyes of Christ, Who sees the dignity and value in each brother and sister. We are citizens of heaven and citizens of the Church, first and foremost.[7] We belong to the whole world, and the whole world is our family (for those in canon law, I am not speaking of juridical territory). Living in this *seminarium* or seedbed of St. Vincent de Paul Regional Seminary is our moment to be healed of prejudices and biases and open ourselves up to the beautiful and multicultural Church and world in which we live.

First of all, what are our prejudices? Prejudice is defined as a "preconceived opinion that is not based on reason or actual experience."[8] In other words, to say that "I do not like that person because he is different from me" is not reasonable. Or to say, "I do not like him because he is a different color, speaks a different language, or comes from a different country" is simply irrational. Growing up in south Louisiana, I witnessed prejudice against people of color. Living in south Florida now, I have seen prejudice among the various Caribbean nations. Can we pretend these realities do not shape our own minds and hearts? A certain amount of arrogance also flows from particular prejudices: "I am better than you because I was born and raised in a particular location and you were not." Prejudice narrows our worldview, as we see people in one dimension or category rather than seeing them in their wholeness.

Even more subtle biases can creep into our minds based on previous experiences. These biases are not fair because they do not give the person in front of us the ability to be different from the person that hurt me in the past. When we lump entire populations together, we leave no room for freedom. For instance, if I had a bad experience with someone from Namibia, and from then on, I project this bias on all Namibians, expecting the same behavior based on my bad experience, I am allowing my past experience to make me prejudiced. We see this all the time in what is referred to as an "implicit bias."

Subtle prejudices and biases—even unconscious racism—can creep in and slowly erode our priestly ministry and the community in which we live. Thus, I invite us all into an

examination of conscience based upon our SVDP Mission
Statement and allow it to form us:

*St. Vincent de Paul Regional Seminary shares in the mission of
Jesus Christ "to bring the good news to the poor" (Luke 4:18) in the
training of future leaders.*

- Do I care for the poor, marginalized, or those
  suffering from discrimination?

- Do I embrace the fullness of the "social doctrine" of
  the Church?

*The seminary's primary mission is to foster the human, spiritual,
intellectual, and pastoral formation of candidates for the Roman Catholic priesthood so that as ordained ministers they share the joy of the
Gospel with all.*

- *With all*—How do I interpret that phrase? The people
  who are like me and my family? Or my parish or
  diocese? Can I or do I love and share the joy of the
  Gospel with all?

*Acknowledging the cultural makeup of Catholics in the United
States, the seminary distinguishes itself in offering a comprehensive
bilingual formation program, preparing future priests for ministry
in both English and Spanish while cultivating a rich and diverse
multicultural community.*

- *Comprehensive bilingual formation program*—Do I take this
  mission seriously or tell myself this does not apply
  to me?

- Do I think that because I live in South Florida, my
  English does not have to be that good, or do I reject
  Spanish out of hardness of heart and think that
  attempting to learn this language does not matter?

- Are we truly a rich and diverse multicultural community, or do we just live in our own silos of language and national groupings, never allowing ourselves really to come into communion with each other?

The secondary mission of St. Vincent de Paul Regional Seminary is to provide graduate theological education for permanent deacon candidates, clergy, religious, and laity, as well as to offer ongoing clergy formation programs so that the evangelizing mission of the Church may continue and broaden its reach.

- Is everything we do about the evangelizing mission of the Church?

- Do I make the connection with the way I live in community now and my future ministry?

Being multiculturally aware, valuing each other's traditions, *and* enculturating ourselves into the land in which we currently live is a gentle balance for each of us at SVDP and the truly Catholic way to live. Let us strive to integrate as a community in an ever-more thorough way; let us ask questions of the person who is "different from me" and strive to understand each other's cultures and backgrounds so we can learn to appreciate the other in the here and now and, thus, our parishioners in the future. We should have a pastoral curiosity about other cultures with a genuine desire to know the other and find fruitful ways to communicate for the sake of community and the sake of our proclamation of the Gospel.

There is also something to be said for having patience with each other when we live in such a diverse house. We all bring our own baggage and biases, not to mention idioms and ways of communicating that can be easily misinterpreted. As a rector with a faculty from eight different countries, I am conscious of these differences and strive to remind myself of this when miscommunications or cultural nuances seem to collide. We are regularly sitting at table with over twenty-five nationalities. We will step on each other's toes sometimes— heck, that is just called being family! It is good to note that some cultural expressions simply do not cross borders, and we must learn to adapt for the sake of communion. For example, burping after a meal in some parts of the world is acceptable and in others, offensive; or our brothers from Africa averting eye contact out of respect have to learn to make eye contact in the United States, or even hugging and kissing on the cheek need to follow the social cues of locality. Know yourself and know your environment, and strive to learn where others are coming from.

Becoming a multicultural community and not just a disparate group of multinationals begins by examining our hearts and having an honest dialogue with our spiritual directors. Our conversion of heart to appreciate each other's traditions and background may necessitate a good confession to be reconciled for any prejudices or hurts that have been subtly clinging to us and affecting our outlook. The healthy multicultural community manifests itself at table in the refectory, on the sports field, and in conversations around the lake. We can certainly see the joy, beauty, and enriching nature of our community on International Night! Certainly, this does not negate the beautiful reality of close friendships and camaraderie with those with whom we share common interests like collegiate background, country of birth, shared hobbies, similitude of personality, and so on. But in community, and simply as Christians, we should always have an openness to the other—to the one who is not like me, the one who is truly my brother or sister though we share little in common. For if I cannot or will not spend time with someone who is different from me now, how will I ever do so in the parish? The parish priest must always remain open to the "other" in his flock or else he will fail to see the "lost sheep" in the lonely, the abandoned, or the confused. Or he will simply fail to preach the Gospel to all who come to him for Good News.

I consider myself truly blessed to have spent years of formation in South Florida. I would never have been exposed to such a rich cultural diversity anywhere else. I would never have been able to embrace the many Latino cultures and the Haitian and Islander nations or have the desire to be able to celebrate the sacraments in Spanish. We miss so much if we do not engage the many cultures around us! It is hard work, but so worth it.

When I arrived at the college seminary in 1991, I spoke zero Spanish; and, to be honest, before arriving, I considered it would be a waste of time because I was from an all-Anglo parish, St. Cecelia's in Clearwater, Florida. But by God's grace and that of many new friends, I immersed myself (as so many of you have) in the new culture and realized the pastoral need of speaking another language and being open to the other.

In the summer of 1996, just five years after entering the seminary, I was on summer assignment at my home parish where I helped launch an outreach program to the burgeoning Spanish-speaking community that had grown in Clearwater. By God's grace, the prejudice I brought with me to the seminary was conquered by the pastoral thirst and curiosity to be the best I could be for the People of God from every background. My best friends at the college seminary were

Cuban, Mexican, and Nicaraguan; and to this day, I remain in close fraternal communion with them. Because of that, I love the big Mass in Miami for La Virgin de La Caridad, Las Mañanitas for Our Lady of Guadalupe, and eating bandeja paisa!

Over the years, I have learned so much that has enriched me from the various Latino cultures and friends from Haiti, the Philippines, the Bahamas, Jamaica, Vietnam, Poland, India, Malta, Nigeria, Ghana, and Kenya. Let us also not fail to mention our need to minister to and embrace the three million Catholic African-Americans[9] who, generally in the South, find themselves underrepresented in our Church. That is why I love meeting black families in the parish and asking about the roots of their Catholic faith. How deficient I would be both personally and pastorally without these friends and their cultures. Worse, how many people would I be depriving of pastoral care if I were closed to cultures outside of my own?

It would never be acceptable in our seminary to marginalize others. I want to raise our awareness because oftentimes, our prejudices are outside of our consciousness; and we need to be reminded to keep asking ourselves about our motivations and to observe our behaviors and words so we grow closer to the ideal of the Christian community where all are valued. We are having this conference tonight not because I believe we are a divided community, but because I know the diabolical (*diabolein*—to scatter or divide) can subtly divide our hearts and fraternity through the experiences of our families and cultures of origin. Let us never give the evil one the upper hand. Let us stand together as one truly Catholic family and stand together as those whose citizenship is in heaven:

"from every nation, race, people, and tongue" (Rev 7:9). May we strive to live in the communion Christ desired for His apostles and still desires for us. For your further reflection, I want to highlight *Canon* 275[10] on the fraternal communion of priests, as well as two passages from John:

> I pray not only for them, but also for those who will believe in me through their word, so that they may all be one, as you, Father, are in me and I in you, that they also may be in us, that the world may believe that you sent me. (Jn 17:20–21)

> I give you a new commandment: love one another. As I have loved you, so you also should love one another. This is how all will know that you are my disciples, if you have love for one another. (Jn 13:34–35)

Let us pray for healing and an end to prejudice and division in our country and in our world as we sing a song that has its origins in the African-American community: "In Christ, there is no East or West."

NOTES

1.   St. Augustine, Sermon "On Pastors," 46 as found in *Liturgy of the Hours*, vol. IV (New York: Catholic Book Publishing Co., 1975), 294.

2.   http://nineteensixty-four.blogspot.com/2010/08/diversification.html (accessed 5/7/19). See also https://en.wikipedia.org/wiki/Catholic_Church_in_the_United_States (accessed 5/7/19).

3.   Ibid.

4.   Ibid.

5.   http://cara.georgetown.edu/.

6.   Francis, "Neighbor to all and Friend of Jesus," Conference to Italian Bishops, (16 May 2016). https://w2.vatican.va/content/francesco/en/speeches/2016/may/documents/papa-francesco_20160516_cei.html (accessed 5/7/19).

7.   See Philippians 3:20.

8.   *Oxford Dictionaries Online*, s.v. "prejudice," https://en.oxforddictionaries.com/definition/prejudice.

9.   Pew Research Center, "A Religious Portrait of African-Americans," (January 30, 2009), http://www.pewforum.org/2009/01/30/a-religious-portrait-of-african-americans/ (accessed 5/7/19).

10.   *Code of Canon Law: Latin-English Edition: New English Translation (Codex Iuris Canonici [CIC])*, (Washington, DC: Canon Law Society of America, 1998), c. 275. See section 1: "Since clerics all work for the same purpose, namely, the building up of the Body of Christ, they are to be united among themselves by a bond of brotherhood and prayer and are to strive for cooperation among themselves according to the prescripts of particular law." See section 2: "Clerics are to acknowledge and promote the mission which the laity, each for his or her part, exercise in the Church and in the world."

The Holy Hour

One of the best decisions I made in 1991, next to entering the seminary, was to pray a daily Holy Hour. It was my first semester at Saint John Vianney College Seminary in Miami, and someone gave me a cassette tape of a talk by the late Archbishop Fulton J. Sheen.[1] In it, Sheen spoke of the absolute and essential nature of his own daily eucharistic Holy Hour (not generally exposition, but adoration of Christ in the tabernacle). As I listened to this great orator speak of this time as the *sine qua non* from which his wisdom flowed, I was inspired by the Holy Spirit at that moment to embrace the same daily habit. Sheen also wrote of this in his autobiography, *Treasure in Clay*, which I highly recommend. In it, he wrote:

> [One] reason I keep up the Holy Hour is to grow more and more into His likeness. As Paul puts it: "We are transfigured into His likeness, from splendor to splendor." We become like that which we gaze upon. Looking into a sunset, the face takes on a golden glow. Looking at the Eucharistic Lord for an hour transforms the heart in a mysterious way as the face of Moses was transformed after his companionship with God on the mountain. Something happens to us similar to that which happened

to the disciples at Emmaus. On Easter Sunday afternoon when the Lord met them, He asked why they were so gloomy. After spending some time in His presence, and hearing again the secret of spirituality—"The Son of Man must suffer to enter into His Glory"—their time with Him ended, and their "hearts were on fire."[2]

I must admit that I did not really know what I was doing or was even supposed to do during the hour—nonetheless, I embraced this daily discipline. Like they say in the rooms of Alcoholics Anonymous, "Fake it till you make it." The analogy of sunbathing has always spoken to me as a Floridian. By doing nothing but sitting in the sun, exposed to the warmth of its rays, we are literally transformed. How much more do the rays of His grace transform us imperceptibly yet significantly as we, day in and day out, sit in the presence of our God incarnate, Jesus Christ present in the tabernacle? We walk out of the chapel not with a suntan, but with the transforming radiance of becoming more like Christ the Light of the World. We know that the saints *radiate Christ*—as do we when we spend time in His presence.

Another analogy that speaks to my heart is of a son spending time with his father. Imperceptibly, the son picks up the traits and habits (for good or ill) of his dad—the way he walks, talks, crosses his legs, and so on. Thus, we begin to imitate Christ the more we spend time with Him in the intimacy of prayer. As the years have gone by, I have learned more about the spiritual life, *lectio divina*, meditation, and a love of silent contemplative prayer; and the Holy Hour has become even more fruitful. However, in the early years—and even in periods of dryness or distraction—growth was always

occurring as I soaked in the Son and sat on the lap of my
Father. Some days, subjectively, the prayer could be better;
but I also believe that objectively, it is always efficacious even
when we "feel" nothing. St. Thérèse gives us some comfort
by reminding us of the Father's delight when we simply fall
asleep in His arms. Who does not love it when a baby falls
asleep as you rock it? However, our aim is not to show up just
to get a good nap, but to grow in relationship with the God
who loves us.

I do not have a perfect attendance award for the daily
Holy Hour, but it is a major priority in my life; and I definitely
have a winning percentage. Again, Fulton Sheen has given me
great inspiration from his daily devotion of being in the presence of Christ in the tabernacle—even to the point of sitting
right outside the Church if it is locked (I have done this many
times myself). That is not to say that one could not pray
elsewhere, like in one's room or out in nature, but Archbishop
Sheen, among others', preference is to try, as far as possible,
to pray in the presence of the Lord in the tabernacle. Think
of our Jewish brothers and sisters who pray at the Western
Wall just because it is the closest they can get to where the
Holy of Holies once was. That is devotion. How much more
so for us when Jesus is waiting for us in the tabernacle! On
the days I do not get there, I can feel a void in my life, and I
make a resolve for the next day to better prioritize that beautiful time of intimacy with the God who loves me.

Statistical data, likewise, proves the Holy Hour to be of
great benefit. Monsignor Steven Rossetti's research has "dem-
onstrated the broad positive effects of prayer in a priest's life.
As priests' time in private prayer increased, they were less
emotionally exhausted, less depressed, less lonely, less likely

to be obese, better able to deal with stress, had an increased sense of inner peace, reported being happier as priests, and had a stronger relationship to God. These increases were consistent with up to an hour of daily private prayer."[3] It should be no real surprise that priests who take the time for personal prayer of up to an hour a day truly experience greater peace and satisfaction in their vocation and in their ministry. The Rossetti study further shows that satisfaction did not increase with multiple hours spent in prayer, so no need to pray three daily Holy Hours as diocesan priests (except on retreat).[4] While that might be a wonderfully pious thought, it is not our particular vocation—we are not monks or hermits. I get the occasional complaint from pastors regarding the overzealous pray-er who is neglecting pastoral duties with an overextended prayer life. Stay balanced, brothers, and remember who you are and what your vocation is all about. *Nosce te ipsum!* That being said, I encourage you to begin the habit now of a daily Holy Hour, or at least begin building up to that. What are the fruits of such a spiritual discipline?

- Increased sensitivity to the promptings of the Holy Spirit because our spiritual senses are used to listen to God in silence.

- Deeper insight into the Word of God, which is made manifest in our preaching and teaching. As St. Vincent de Paul wrote: "Only by praying does one touch people's hearts when one proclaims the Gospel."[5]

- A calmer heart and well-ordered mind because we learn to rest in God. John 15 comes to mind about remaining in His love. This deep place of intimacy is where we turn to the Father for healing, comfort, and strength.

- An intimate place of being known by the Other. This is all about our relationship with God, the most important relationship in our lives—and in a particular way as celibate men.

- Space where we can acknowledge our grief, suffering, and pain in order to be healed.[6]

- Finally, prayer is also the place where our hearts grow and we fall more and more in love with God and His holy people. "The fruit of prayer is love," as Mother Teresa so often would say. Do not gauge the "success" of our daily prayer by what happens during that time, but by how we are acting when not in prayer.[7]

Likewise, Pope Francis recently shared his thoughts on the fruit of our daily prayer time adoring Our Lord:

One who adores, who takes up the living wellspring of love cannot but be left, so to speak, "contaminated." And he begins to behave with others as the Lord does with him: he becomes more merciful, more understanding, more willing; he overcomes his own rigidity and opens himself to others.[8]

I believe this daily time, whether in the form of one continuous hour or broken up through the day, to be indispensable for our active and pastoral lifestyle. We will not do it perfectly. And sometimes, the time will get "filled up" by catching up with a couple "hours" of the Divine Office (which, of course, is a promise we make and is *not* optional!) or writing our next two homilies or talks. But my goal is to have at least half of the time for true silent prayer. There may even be days we might miss the Holy Hour, but if the Holy Hour is not a daily goal or a recognized need, it will not make it into our schedule. In fact, a good way to stay accountable is to let loved ones know this is part of your daily routine, so whether you are visiting family, traveling, or with friends on vacation, it remains a part of your daily routine.

Silence is so important for our hearts and souls. Silence is a dialogue in which we listen for the voice of God and allow Him to be present to us in the noisiness of our lives (remember to turn the phone to airplane mode). The Holy Father said this about spending silent moments with Jesus:

> From this mysterious silence of God springs his Word which resonates in our heart. Jesus himself teaches us how it is truly possible to "be" with the Father and he shows us this with his prayer. The Gospels show us Jesus who withdraws to secluded places to pray; seeing his intimate relationship with God, the disciples feel the desire to be able to take part in it and they ask him: "Lord, teach us to pray" (Lk 11:1). . . .
>
> Do we have this longing? Does each of us have the wish to be born anew in order to meet the Lord? Do you have this wish? Indeed, one can easily lose it because, due to so many activities, so many projects to implement, in the end we are short of time and we lose sight of what is fundamental: the inner life of the heart, our spiritual life, our life which is the encounter with the Lord in prayer."[9]

Back on December 1, 2017, I was speaking with Bishop Felipe J. Estévez about writing this talk, and he shared with me that it was the anniversary of Brother Charles de Foucauld's death (1916), who was killed while adoring the Blessed Sacrament. The bishop went on to say: "I owe great gratitude in my priestly life to the Jesu Caritas Fraternity, for when I was invited to join, I began the practice of one hour of daily adoration and a monthly desert day. These two charisms have had a huge impact on my journey. Needless to say what the fraternity has meant." I share this with Bishop Estévez's permission, and I do so that we might draw inspiration from his example and the witness of so many saints of yesterday and today who have made prayer a priority in their lives. When Archbishop Sheen would preach priest retreats, he would begin by stating that the only outcome he desired on the retreat was for the participants to take on the practice of a daily Holy Hour.

For Christmas, I gave you a book about seven habits of highly effective people[10] because I want you to soar as leaders and shepherds of the communities entrusted to your care, but you will do so only if you are grounded in prayer. I beg you to make good New Year's resolutions flowing from your retreats to draw ever closer to the Lord on a daily basis. And so today, I offer you the "Seven Habits of Highly Effective Priests":

1. Participating in daily Mass

2. Praying the Liturgy of the Hours

3. Offering a Holy Hour

4. Having devotion to the Blessed Mother

5. Attending monthly spiritual direction

6.   Going on an annual retreat

7.   Staying in fraternity with your brother priests

By forming these habits now, I assure you that you will become "highly effective" and that these daily, monthly, and annual spiritual habits will greatly enrich your personal and pastoral life "for our good and the good of all His Holy Church!"

NOTES

1. Sensus Fidelium. "Ven Fulton Sheen: Holy Hour of Adoration," *YouTube* video, 41:46 (July 5, 2016). https://www.youtube.com/watch?v=YT-vzobvYMg (accessed Feb. 6, 2019).
2. Fulton J. Sheen, *Treasure in Clay: The Autobiography of Fulton J. Sheen* (New York: Doubleday, 1980), 188-189.
3. Stephen J. Rossetti, *Why Priests are Happy: A Study of the Psychological and Spiritual Health of Priests* (Notre Dame, IN: Ave Maria Press, 2011), 11.
4. Ibid.
5. St. Vincent de Paul, as referenced by Pope Francis, *Address to the Vincentian Family on the Fourth Centenary of the Charism (2017)*. https://w2.vatican.va/content/francesco/en/speeches/2017/october/documents/papa-francesco_20171014_famiglia-vincenziana.html (accessed 5/7/19).
6. See James Keating, "Giving Our Grief Over to the 'Man Acquainted with Grief,'" *Homiletic and Pastoral Review*. https://www.hprweb.com/2014/06/giving-our-grief-over-to-the-man-acquainted-with-grief/ (accessed 6/11/2019).
7. See 1 Corinthians 13.
8. Francis, *Address to the Vincentian Family on the Fourth Centenary of the Charism* (14 October 2017), para. 7.
9. Francis, *General Audience* (15 November 2017), para. 5, 8.
10. See Steven R. Covey, *The 7 Habits of Highly Effective People* (New York: Free Press, 1989).

FREEDOM

One of the most iconic movie scenes of the 1990s was in *Braveheart* when William Wallace (played by Mel Gibson) led his war-painted thirteenth century Scottish Highlanders with the battle cry "Freedom!"[1] This should also be the cry of *our* hearts, and certainly my desire for each of you: to live in total and absolute freedom as you discern God's call for your life. Please be aware of anything that can hinder your freedom to choose and be chosen by God. Are any areas obstacles for you?

To the extent that you are comfortable, I encourage you to discuss any obstacles in spiritual direction and formation, advising the staff any time you feel suffocated or unfree in your life here in the seminary. We do not and cannot force you to do anything. If you experience the rules of the seminary as truly oppressive—and I am not talking about the occasional challenge—then discuss that with your spiritual director and formation advisor. To paraphrase the vice rector, it could be "a positive sign . . . of *another* vocation."

You do not *have* to do anything! Our free choice now to submit ourselves to authority is preparation for the life we have chosen and are being chosen for. The Church is not forcing you to be a celibate, obedient, prayerful, public figure.

<u>You are freely choosing this, and after you make that choice</u>
<u>at ordination, that choice is for life</u>!

We see such total freedom in our newly beatified martyr
Blessed Stanley Rother,[2] whose total freedom bound him
to the fate of his people. He was determined to give his
life completely to his flock in Guatemala, stating that "the
shepherd cannot run."[3] One of his priest friends testified
that, had Father Stan not returned to Guatemala, "he would
have survived, but he certainly would have not lived!"[4] In his
last Christmas letter, Father Stan wrote home to his bishop
in Oklahoma: "If it is my destiny that I should give my life
here, then so be it."[5] Right before Holy Week, he spoke with
his local bishop in Guatemala and assured him: "My life is
for my people. I am not scared."[6] This is freedom! This is a
freedom grounded in the freest man ever to live: Jesus Christ!
Jesus was so free because His only desire was to do the will
of the Father.

Sometimes we might hear grumblings like: "But it is too
hard to do what is asked of me all the time!" or "I don't want
to do all this stuff, and I don't want to be a public person; I
want to be a priest on my own terms!" To quote the movie
Apollo 13: "Houston, we have a problem!"[7] Deacon Jim Keating shared a great image with me. When his son approached
his future father-in-law to ask for his daughter's hand in
marriage, he did not quite get the exuberant response that he
expected. His future father-in-law questioned him on how
he would provide for his daughter and as to what kind of
husband he would be. Upon his return home he told Jim,
"Well, he didn't throw me a parade." Certainly, that is because
a father wants to make sure his daughter, the bride, is taken
care of and provided for by the groom. The bride is not so

desperate that she will just take anyone, and the father knows the giftedness of his daughter.

In a way, seminary formators are like the father-in-law just mentioned. Our job is to protect the Bride, the Church. Marriage must be entered into freely and without reservation. Our job is to ensure that you are ready to embrace the Bride by the time you approach ordination; thus, formation advising and annual evaluations are so important. We can understand the analogy used here if we think about what the bride and groom must know about each other to enter into marriage freely—without reservation or duress. Be free in sharing with the Church everything that your Bride needs to know about you. That is what formation advising is all about. A groom does not go to his bride for confession, and there are some things she simply does not need to know—save that for spiritual direction. But grow in transparency with the Church, and you will experience greater freedom.

Some seminarians go through six to nine years of formation living in fear of getting kicked out—that is not of God, nor is it a peaceful place of freedom to live. Live in freedom. A prayer of mine in seminary was: "God, you called me here. If You want me to be a priest, I give You permission to lead me there. If You do not, please close the door and open others." Trust the Holy Spirit to lead *you*, and trust the Holy Spirit to lead *us* in helping you as well. I think it is important to point out that we do not like to "kick people out." In fact, I wish every seminarian were a man of integrity and became a wonderful, holy, hardworking missionary disciple. According to the Center for Applied Research in the Apostolate (CARA), the reality is that at least 25 percent of you will depart seminary formation at some point in the journey, and we all need to acknowledge that this is a normal part of the process. You are not a failure if you discern out or are asked to leave—we are not failures on the seminary level either—it simply means formation works. The reason seminary is so long is because discernment and formation take time. Remember, there are two discernments occurring: the seminarian's and the Church's.[8]

It is important to note that freedom works both ways. The bride is as free as the groom. The Church needs to have freedom in her discernment, as does the seminarian in his. So, let us talk openly about what happens when the Church—the task of ecclesial discernment of the seminary—asks someone to leave. I want to shine light on the process so you realize that we do not act indiscriminately or in isolation. Now, do not panic: I had to give a talk a month ago at the National Vocation Director gathering on the topic of dismissals, so I thought it opportune to share some of these thoughts with you as well. A dismissal may happen in two ways. The first one is a dismissal of urgent necessity due to a particular moral failure or circumstance. The second is also a dismissal of necessity but is not urgent; it is due to an inability of the seminarian to embrace or respond to the program of priestly formation appropriately.

The first kind of dismissal is the most serious but, ironically, may be the easiest. If the man has been caught in an egregious act with verifiable evidence, the seminary and the diocese should act promptly in offering a swift dismissal. It is important for you to know that I meet with all parties involved, listen to all sides, collect information, pray for wisdom and discernment, and trust the Holy Spirit to make manifest what needs to come to light, and then move and act as needed. I also do not make any decisions without serious consultation with the formation team, the diocesan vocation director, and the bishop. Whenever I need to discuss something very serious, I invite the formation advisor, the spiritual director, and the seminarian to my office to make sure that everyone hears the same thing—clarity and lack of ambiguity or triangulation is important at this point.

A dismissal occurs if someone has broken a serious moral boundary, such as stealing or flagrant plagiarism. But more often, dismissal occurs from something of a relational nature with another person, such as dating, sexual activity, or serious boundary violations. Remember, we are called to live in freedom, but not a freedom that gives free rein to the flesh. As St. Paul writes: "For you were called for freedom, brothers. But do not use this freedom as an opportunity for the flesh; rather, serve one another through love. . . . Live by the Spirit and you will certainly not gratify the desire of the flesh" (Gal 5:13, 16). Know you are free to do whatever you desire, but also remember there are consequences. No one is dismissed unless it is a grave matter, and these decisions are made with serious discernment and due process. However, I understand it is very hard when a friend is dismissed and you most likely have incomplete information. Please know that we cannot share that information with you or the community for the sake of the man's reputation. (You can get a release form if you want because as our professor of canon law will remind us: *Canon* 220 states that "no one is permitted to harm illegitimately the good reputation which a person possesses nor to injure the right of any person to protect his or her own privacy."[9])

The second kind of dismissal happens when the seminarian simply does not have the requisite qualities for the diocesan priesthood in the twenty-first century. As the *Program of Priestly Formation* states:

> Seminarians who lack the positive qualities for continuing in formation should not be advanced in the seminary program. They should be advised to leave the seminary. Seminarians not recommended for advancement should be notified as early as possible and in a constructive manner. In these cases, an opportunity should be provided for the seminarian to present his self-assessment; others who can speak on the seminarian's behalf should also be heard.[10]

As we like to say, formation is not meant to be an "Easter egg hunt"—we should not have to work that hard to see priestly virtues and qualities in you; they should be manifestly self-evident. If, after many advising sessions and repeated efforts to assist a seminarian in his growth, including the possibility of growth counseling or even a warning of formation probation, he still shows no sign or an insufficient amount of needed growth, then the formation team will come to an impasse on the path forward and must assist the man, erring always on the side of the Church, to move out of priestly formation. We strive never to surprise a man about areas of needed growth, but rather address them immediately so he has a real opportunity to grow and show us the needed change. However, growth does not always happen, and then we can be at peace knowing we have given the seminarian every opportunity for growth and change prior to dismissal. The *Program of Priestly Formation* further states:

When there is doubt about the readiness of a seminarian for advancement, consideration can be given to a recommendation of a period of probation outside the seminary. The time period involved should be specified, not open-ended. The period of probation should have clearly identified goals and means to assess the achievement of goals. Likewise, appropriate supervision is necessary so that this period away would help bring about needed growth for a possible return to the seminary. If doubts remain after this period, the seminarian should not continue in formation.[11]

That being said, I have seen miracles and quantum leaps occur in a man's vocational journey at the point of being challenged by the seminary, which in my mind is always the preferable outcome! Sadly, others "just don't have it"—they do not possess the requisite qualities for priestly ministry today. In such a case, we work very hard to help the seminarian see that the priesthood is simply not a fit. This is particularly difficult if the man does not see that. At that point, we review with him the two forms of discernment occurring—the personal and the ecclesial (as previously mentioned)—explaining that the Church does not see the requisite qualities for his advancement.

It is also very challenging if there is a borderline issue or the seminarian does not accept the subtle and not-so-subtle guidance of his formation advisor and/or the rector. Working with a seminarian who has done nothing "wrong," but whom we do not believe "has it" or will be "useful for ministry"[12] can be most difficult. We strive to be gentle and kind as we accompany the man on this journey, mindful that we are dealing with a soul. This process does not happen overnight; it takes lots of discernment and time to unfold. If priesthood is not a fit for a man, then the reality is that *he* will never be happy or content in his life. In the end, we are actually trying to help him discover his true vocation in Christ. It is ultimately an act of charity toward him, even though he may not see it at the time.

The formation team often resorts to "four formation factors" as a way to help us gauge a man's possibility for progress:

1. Gauge the seriousness of the issues: Are they hurting the Church versus being annoying or idiosyncratic?

2. Gauge the time expected for the issues to be resolved: short-term versus long-term versus lifelong.

3. Gauge the capacity of the individual to accomplish the desired change and/or resolution.

4. Gauge the willingness of the individual to enter into the desired change (influenced by past track record).

The Holy Spirit is in charge, and we need to allow Him to inspire and lead us when tough decisions are to be made. The seminary must always err on the side of the Bride. The benefit of the doubt must always go to the Church. Two questions I often ask are: "Would I want this man as my associate pastor?" and "Would I want him in my sister's parish?" If the answer to either of these questions is "no," then we are called to act. The seminary, like the father-in-law, gives no free rides—formation is not a parade; it is hard work! The Bride of Christ deserves only men who embrace daily conversion and transformation in a true spirit of freedom so genuine formation can occur.

On the flip side, it is important for the seminary faculty to regularly remind you that you should not live in fear of being dismissed. Live in freedom! If it is God's will for you to become ordained, it will happen. If it is not, we pray that He make it clear to you and us because we all want the Father's will for your lives. It is never our desire to dismiss seminarians; but at times, it is necessary. It is never indiscriminate. We certainly do not sit around and say, "We already have too many priests; let's mess with this guy and play games." I want to encourage you to trust and be transparent—the seminarian who is transparent, humble, and open to formation has nothing to fear and will experience a great sense of freedom. I have seen this and know it is true!

If you do not want to live in the way the seminary and the Church demand, then please depart. No one is forcing you to stay! The deacon's homily last Monday spoke also of the affirming nature of the Church's discernment on your behalf. When you are in doubt, be open to those entrusted with your formation to help you. The rector, the formation advisor, and the diocese should not be the last to know of your decision to depart seminary formation but should be part of the process of discernment—that is only a matter of fairness to your fiancée.

The etched marble wall at the Korean War Memorial in Washington, D.C., states quite starkly: "Freedom is not free!" Our freedom costs us our lives. "Yet I live, no longer I, but Christ lives in me" (Gal 2:20). Our truest freedom is a surrender to live completely for Christ and His Church. The freedom that binds us actually makes us ever more free! Free to give ourselves joyfully in poverty, chastity, and obedience. Free to realize the seminary is not a cakewalk or a parade (nor is the priesthood going to be easy!) but a time to struggle through difficulties and be transformed—a time of configuration to Christ who came to serve and not be served!

The seminary wants to enrich your freedom by helping you become ever more aware of your own contradictions and more open to wholesome living. The seminary faculty want to help you close the distance between the ideal and your reality year by year, free to live in trust, transparency, authenticity, and humility as we each desire to grow in relationship with Jesus Christ, the freest man to ever live! William Wallace knew life would be tough and the fight for freedom might well cost him his life; but he was free, and that allowed him to sacrifice everything. This is also the freedom a priest must possess to live and minister like Father Stanley Rother. And that is the life of freedom the Lord desires for each of us.

Pope Francis constantly reminds us that everything is about Christ:

> How can we discover our own vocation in this world? It can be discovered in many ways, but . . . the first indicator is the joy of the encounter with Jesus. . . . [E]very true vocation begins with an encounter with Jesus who gives us joy and hope anew; and he leads us, even through trials and difficulties, to an ever fuller encounter; that encounter with him, grows greater, and to the fullness of joy.[13]

As St. Paul writes: "For freedom Christ set us free; so stand firm and do not submit again to the yoke of slavery" (Gal 5:1).

NOTES

1. See the speech in this clip: "Braveheart: Freedom Speech," in *Braveheart*, dir. Mel Gibson, perf. Mel Gibson (USA: Twentieth Century Fox Film Corporation, 1995), film, May 9, 2013, by Fox Home Entertainment UK, https://www.youtube.com/watch?v=hIvRkjOd1f8.

2. For those of you who are unfamiliar with Blessed Stanley Rother, I encourage you to learn more about him here: http://stanleyrother.org/about/.

3. "About Blessed Stanley Rother," Archdiocese of Oklahoma, Blessed Stanley Rother, para. 12, http://stanleyrother.org/about/.

4. "An Ordinary Martyr: The Life and Death of Blessed Stanley Rother," by the Archdiocese of Oklahoma, https://www.youtube.com/watch?v=55y77RA3_eA (accessed 5/7/19).

5. Ibid.

6. Ibid.

7. See the speech in this clip: "Apollo 13 (1995) – Houston, We Have a Problem (4/11)," in *Apollo 13*, dir. Ron Howard, perf. Tom Hanks, Bill Paxton, and Kevin Bacon (USA: Universal Pictures, Imagine Entertainment, 1995), film, Aug 3, 2017, by Fandango Movieclips https://www.youtube.com/watch?v=C3J1AO9z0tA.

8. See the booklet on personal and ecclesial discernment by Jim Shae, *Discernment within the Heart of the Church: A Helpful Guide for the Diocesan Seminarian* (Huntington, NY: National Conference of Diocesan Vocation Directors, n.d.).

9. *Code of Canon Law: Latin-English Edition: New English Translation (Codex Iuris Canonici [CIC])*, (Washington, DC: Canon Law Society of America, 1998), c. 220.

10. United States Conference of Catholic Bishops, *Program of Priestly Formation*, 5th ed. (Washington, DC: USCCB, 2006), sec. 287.

11. Ibid., sec. 288.

12. *CIC*, c. 1025, sec. 2.

13. Francis, *General Audience* (30 August 2017), para. 5. https://w2.vatican.va/content/francesco/en/audiences/2017/documents/papa-francesco_20170830_udienza-generale.html (accessed 5/7/19).

MEN OF COMMUNION

Men of Communion. We hear this phrase regularly, but what does it mean? Literally, it means to be "in union." In union with *what* or, better, with *whom*? Simply put, in union with God and others. This communion can be thought of as both vertical and horizontal—both being essential. "This is our highest vocation: to enter into communion with God and with our brothers and sisters."[1] This communion begins in Baptism when we were made "sharers in the divine nature" (2 Pt 1:4) with the indwelling of the Blessed Trinity. This communion is meant to be a living relationship.

Flowing from our communion with God is our communion with the Church—we are to be witnesses to ecclesial communion,[2] and in particular, building the presbyteral unity begins now. Am I open to my brothers? Am I in union with them, even if they are different from me—old, young, liberal, conservative, Latino, Polish, African, fat, skinny, black, white, and so on? The presbyterates of our dioceses are a motley crew, beginning with ourselves. We have just returned from Holy Week and the beautiful symbolism of the Chrism Mass in which we renew our priestly commitment and concelebrate with our bishop. This is communion—being open to the other, especially our elders.[3] Priesthood is a bond of most intimate communion. For example, the priest faculty spans a fifty-year differential in birth, priestly formation, and ordination—not to mention, we represent seven different national backgrounds, not counting Pensacola!—yet we deeply love and respect each other regardless of differences in style. In fact, we all had a hand in writing this conference!

This bond must be fostered now by actively engaging in communion, in particular with regard to spirituality and common prayer. Such moments in the Eucharist, the Liturgy of the Hours, adoration, and diocesan nights bind us together. Two definitions from the Church of what it means to be men of communion will help us. The first is from St. John Paul II and the second is from the *Program of Priestly Formation*. St. John Paul II wrote:

> Of special importance is the capacity to relate to others. This is truly fundamental for a person who is called to be responsible for a community and to be a "man of communion." This demands that the priest not be arrogant or quarrelsome, but affable, hospitable, sincere in his words and heart, prudent and discreet, generous and ready to serve, capable of opening himself to clear and brotherly relationships and of encouraging the same in others, and quick to understand, forgive, and console.[4]

And the *Program of Priestly Formation* reminds us:

> *A man of communion*: a person who has real and deep relational capacities, someone who can enter into genuine dialogue and friendship, a person of true empathy who can understand and know other persons, a person open to others and available to them with a generosity of spirit. The man of communion is capable of making a gift of

himself and of receiving the gift of others. This, in fact, requires the full possession of oneself. This life should be one of inner joy and inner peace—signs of self-possession and generosity.[5]

The man of communion lives the beautiful litany of First Corinthians 13: desiring always the good of the other through patience and kindness, never delighting in the downfall of the other but in the building up of the body of Christ. "Thus community becomes '*Schola Amoris*,' a School of Love."[6] If you cannot love here, how will you love in the parish? This is the time and place! How often I hear from a seminarian who is being challenged to grow by the formation team that we should see him in the parish because there, he is filled with charity, joy, and sacrificial love. My response is: "Please invite that man to live here. This is your parish!" Men of communion do not compete against each other—except to be first in offering forgiveness. Being jealous of and conspiring against each other often flows from having listened in our hearts to fears of our own inadequacies. Give each other the benefit of the doubt and presume good intentions. The man of communion also knows how to easily laugh at himself; this is affective maturity.

The document "Fraternal Life in Community" offers us a vision of what Christian communion should look like based on scriptural citations—in other words, this is not just for religious:

Every day, communities take up again their journey, sustained by the teaching of the Apostles: "love one another with brotherly affection; outdo one another in showing honor" (Rom. 12:10); "live in harmony with one

another" (Rom. 12:16); "welcome one another, therefore,
as Christ has welcomed you" (Rom. 15:7); "I myself am
satisfied . . . that you are . . . able to instruct one another"
(Rom. 15:14); "wait for one another" (1 Cor. 11:33);
"through love, be servants of one another" (Gal. 5:13);
"encourage one another" (1 Thes. 5:11); "forbearing one
another in love" (Eph. 4:2); "be kind to one another,
tender-hearted, forgiving one another" (Eph. 4:32); "be
subject to one another out of reverence for Christ"
(Eph. 5:21); "pray for one another" (James 5:16); "clothe
yourselves, all of you, with humility towards one another"
(1 Pet. 5:5); "we have fellowship with one another" (1 Jn.
1:7); "let us not grow weary in well-doing . . . ,
especially to those who are of the household of faith"
(Gal. 6:9–10). . . .

It may be useful to recall that in order to foster
communion of minds and hearts among those called
to live together in a community, it is necessary to
cultivate those qualities which are required in all human
relationships: respect, kindness, sincerity, self-control,
tactfulness, a sense of humor and a spirit of sharing.[7]

This is how we must strive to live now and one day model
in our parishes and rectories, for both evangelization and
vocations hinge on this witness. Our joy lived in the community of the rectory and the parish invites others into the love
of Christ:

A joyless fraternity is one that is dying out; before long,
members will be tempted to seek elsewhere what they
can no longer find within their own home. A fraternity
rich in joy is a genuine gift from above to brothers and

sisters who know how to ask for it and to accept one another, committing themselves to fraternal life, trusting in the action of the Spirit. Thus the words of the Psalm are made true: "Behold how good and pleasant it is when brothers dwell in unity" . . . (Ps. 133:1-3).[8]

Communion through communication! Have openness to the other. Hosting regular gatherings and meetings is all important! We grow in communion as we communicate in even the simplest of ways. Every genuine human encounter is a moment of growth in relationship. Living in community (rectory living) means telling the other what you are doing; we are accountable to each other. Dialogue with each other, and truly listen in order to understand where your brother is coming from (emotionally, existentially, and ecclesially). No more lone rangers—"I did it my way" is not our theme song (apologies to Sinatra). We are to be men of communion with each other. We are responsible to and for each other. St. John Paul II noted that the ordained ministry has a radical "communitarian form" and can only be carried out as a "collective work."[9]

We need to understand what a real human relationship is and means. How do we learn to communicate in depth, in complement, and in continuity? What goes into forming lifelong friendships and friendships that open out to others? The meal is the privileged place of such communication and communion. Say "No" to technology at the table! Reaching out to form relationships (not just acquaintances) with all in the community means not racing in and out of the dining room or saving places so that you can *always* sit with your special friends. It also means not regularly doing "Chinese takeout" with the Styrofoam trays from the refectory—this should only be done on the rarest of occasions; after all, our meals really do not take that long.

Community is also the place of formation—where our rough edges are meant to be dulled in the crucible of community, much like how iron sharpens iron. This process can be demanding and challenging. How do we treat each other and care for each other? By God's grace, we are an amazing community, and so much good happens here on a daily basis. But are we open to the kind of ongoing conversion Pope Francis has spoken of eloquently and powerfully concerning conversion as changing the way we think? This, I believe, is the foundational action of formation. The ancient sense of the "conversion of manners," that is, taking on the heart and mind of Christ, still can slip from the center of our attention. I encourage each of us to be more consciously intentional in building on what we are already doing. Our hospitality is great, but to use an example we have used before, do we consciously step back to make sure our guests go before us at the dining buffet line? This sense of welcoming and hospitality will one day either make your parish a thriving family-focused environment or, if ignored, a cold parish serving as a sacramental conveyer belt. Christ wants more! Our goal is to be intentional and conscious in making the link to future ministry as men of communion. Am I thinking and then acting as Christ? Some of our twentieth century favorites did this very well: St. Maximilian Kolbe, Blessed Pier Giorgio Frassati, and St. John Paul II, to name just a few.

In this multicultural community, which all our parishes will be as well, we must ask: Am I sensitive and open to the other? Am I aware of subtle social patterns that can slip into table conversation or prejudicial comments or jokes that are derogatory to others? The new *Ratio Fundamentalis* states that the future priest is "called above all to a basic human and spiritual serenity that, by overcoming every form of self-promotion, or emotional dependency, allows him to be a man of communion, of mission, and of dialogue."[10] We need men of communion, of mission, and of dialogue in the Church now more than ever!

Please do not forget the first community from which we came, our families. We should be men of communion with those to whom we are related—sometimes this is very easy, and sometimes this can be very difficult. Also be conscious of forming relationships of communion with other families and staying grounded in the reality of how our parishioners live and struggle. My own experience of being in Teams of Our Lady with five married couples over the past eighteen years has deeply enriched my life as a priest. Families such as these, and in fact all the faithful, need us to form the necessary virtues to be men of communion. This broadens our hearts to be able to reach out, in the words of Pope Francis, to the "existential peripheries." I think of our Christmas mission trip to Haiti and what it meant to the people we visited and to those who went. What mattered most was the sense of "solidarity and presence"; being "in communion" with the Haitians was more important than anything we did.

Thus, I want to review four enemies that can plague us in our lifelong journey to grow in communion with God and others:

1. Inadequacy or fear of being inadequate. This enemy of communion leads us constantly to compare

ourselves with others and judge ourselves unworthy and inadequate, impotent for the mission. I remember arriving for my first year in the seminary and comparing myself to my classmates and realizing the men around me were smarter, more athletic, more personable, and holier than I was. Ouch! I had to learn to rejoice in my brothers' gifts as well as discover my own. If we do not surrender these feelings to the Lord, we will be left with disappointment that leads to discouragement that leads to doubt that leads to despair. Do not go there!

2. Isolation. When we remove ourselves from communion with God and community life, we can become isolated here in the seminary; and it can certainly happen in the parish. When we forget we are beloved sons and brothers, we lose our sense of belonging to Christ and to those around us. We might escape by locking ourselves in our rooms and binging on Netflix, pornography, or even online shopping! We have been created in the image and likeness of God who is relational. When we remain in relationship, we are drawn from darkness into His life-giving light.

3. Cynicism. Brothers, negativity destroys community— in the seminary, in the presbyterate, and in the parish. Cynicism breeds disunity and distrust. I do not need to say more; we all know what it looks like. If you struggle with this demon, bring it to spiritual direction and formation advising; wrestle with this poison in order conquer it in Christ. Again, know who you are. Your identity as a beloved son of the Father and a universal brother changes everything.

4.   Suspicion. If I live with a "hermeneutic of suspicion"
     about those around me, I am really going to be
     miserable, not to mention fearful and paranoid. This
     can easily happen with our colleagues and superiors.
     Learn how to trust God in genuine humility, and
     everything else falls into place. If I trust in the
     Father to lead me, I can then trust in Him working
     through all situations.[11] Strive to live a hermeneutic
     of continuity and communion with your bishop, the
     faculty, your brother seminarians, and the priests
     of our diocese to avoid marginalizing yourself
     and others.

Remember that communion with God and others is
always aimed at service and pastoral charity—our lives are to
be about others! I want to conclude with the reality of Holy
Communion as *the* point of integration. Because the Eucharist is the "source and summit" of our relationship with God
and the model for the purification of our relationships and
those within the parish, as we receive Holy Communion at
each Mass, may we be reminded that we are to live in deep
communion with the Triune God and all those around us.

To be a man of communion is the idea of being a "man
for others" that we hear repeated at every Mass: "this is
my Body which will be given up for you. . . . my Blood . . .
poured out for you." Being a man of communion is at the
center of our worship, of our mission. This action and the
words of Jesus lead to our communion with Him and with
others and stand as a constant reminder of who we are as
men of communion. Pope Benedict XVI reflected on this
Christ/communion dimension:

His entire being is expressed by the word, "pro-existence"—he is there, not for himself but for others. This is not merely a dimension of his existence, but its innermost essence and its entirety. His very being is a "being-for." If we are able to grasp this, then we have truly come close to the mystery of Jesus, and we have understood what discipleship is."[12]

NOTES

1. Congregation for Institutes of Consecrated Life and Societies of Apostolic Life, "Fraternal Life in Community," (2 February 1994), sec. 9. http://www.vatican.va/roman_curia/congregations/ccscrlife/documents/rc_con_ccscrlife_doc_02021994_fraternal-life-in-community_en.html (accessed 5/7/19).
2. See John 17 and Acts 2:42.
3. See chapter 2 of David L. Toups, *Reclaiming Our Priestly Character*, rev. ed. (Omaha, NE: The Insitute for Priestly Formation, 2010).
4. John Paul II, *Pastores Dabo Vobis* (1992), sec. 43.
5. United States Conference of Catholic Bishops (USCCB), *Program of Priestly Formation*, 5th ed. (Washington DC: USCCB, 2006), sec. 76. Emphasis in original.
6. Congregation for Institutes of Consecrated Life and Societies of Apostolic Life, "Fraternal Life in Community," sec. 25. Emphasis in original.
7. Ibid., sec. 26–27.
8. Ibid., sec. 28.
9. *Pastores Dabo Vobis*, sec. 17.
10. Congregation for the Clergy, *The Gift of the Priestly Vocation* (Vatican City: L'Osservatore Romano, 2016), sec. 41.
11. See Romans 8:28.
12. Joseph Ratzinger, *Jesus of Nazareth: Holy Week: From the Entrance into Jerusalem to the Resurrection* (San Francisco: Ignatius Press, 2011), 134.

The Self-Referential Seminarian/Priest

In his reflections to the College of Cardinals prior to being elected to the Papacy, Cardinal Jorge Mario Bergoglio reflected upon the fact that the Church is not herself when she becomes self centered and turned in on herself in a kind of "theological narcissism." He continued, "When the Church does not come out of herself to evangelize, she becomes self-referential and then gets sick."[1]

Pope Francis paints a very clear picture of the kind of seminarian and priest we are to be, and one thing that we should *not* be is self-referential. The world does not revolve around us; this is the way a child lives his life. While we are called to be childlike, we are certainly not called to be childish or, as one author writes, the priest can fall into the trap of remaining a *puer aeternus*—an eternal child or a Peter Pan who never wants to grow up, thus avoiding real responsibility.[2]

We must be careful of narcissistic or individualistic behaviors and tendencies—a real danger for each of us. Pope Francis writes in *Evangelii Gaudium*:

Today we are seeing in many pastoral workers, including consecrated men and women, an inordinate concern for their personal freedom and relaxation, which leads them to see their work as a mere appendage to their life, as if it were not part of their very identity. At the same time, the spiritual life comes to be identified with a few religious exercises which can offer a certain comfort but which do not encourage encounter with others, engagement with the world or a passion for evangelization. As a result, one can observe in many agents of evangelization, even though they pray, a heightened individualism, a crisis of identity and a cooling of fervour. These are three evils which fuel one another.[3]

Please read up on the increasing problem of narcissism in our society and thus, by association, the priesthood. We are not lone rangers; we need to work together as a team and not in isolation. Fraternal collaboration is key. We are called to serve the needs of the parish as enunciated by the pastor—serve your pastor, and try to build him up in front of his people; remember, he stays for the long-haul, and you are there for a much shorter assignment. Do not fall prey to divisions in the parish. With parishioners, keep your opinions to yourself, especially regarding the pastor. There is an arrogance in our fallen human nature that, if not kept in check, can take over our personality and lead us to believe we have all the answers and everyone around us is leading the Church in error.

At times, I hear of newly-ordained priests doing their own thing and taking as their motto Frank Sinatra's, "I did it my way!" Priests and seminarians are assigned by the bishop to serve a particular parish community as their first responsibility, not as a "priest at large." Never take on anything outside of the parish without first talking it through with your pastor to ensure it does not conflict with your responsibilities at home. Be humble enough to be denied at times—do not be a crybaby. Trust those in authority over us, and do what we are supposed to do in both the little and the big things.

On Holy Thursday of 2014, Pope Francis spoke to us about the pitfalls of being "unctuous, sumptuous, and presumptuous"—in other words, becoming self-referential pastors. Tonight, I will elaborate on these three vices.

Unctuous

We are anointed in Baptism, Confirmation, and priesthood to become Christ to the world. The chrism is meant to sink deeply into our souls and transform our lives. However, sometimes the oil remains only on the surface and does not penetrate to the core of our being. Being unctuous happens when our anointing goes awry. The sacred chrism is meant to affect us in the deepest recesses of our hearts and souls—to be Christ at all times. If the oil remains only on the surface, we remain insincere and lacking in integrity. We are to be the same on the inside as we are on the outside. Or do we have, as the TV show is called, *Arrested Development*—or stunted growth in the area of human formation? Do we simply play a role and wear the mask of being a holy person without really desiring to have the heart of the Good Shepherd?

Use your time wisely while you are in formation to allow the risen Christ to heal you: of family of origin dysfunctions, of sinful memories and habits, of unresolved issues. Delve deeply into all this in prayer, spiritual direction, and growth counseling, if needed. If not healed, we will operate out of our own hurts and angers, and perpetuate the same dysfunctions that originally hurt us in the lives of our parishioners.

The self-referential, oily, smarmy, or unctuous priest lacks the sincerity and integrity needed in the mature Christian and minister of the Church.

Sumptuous

We become sumptuous when we become too comfortable in our lifestyle. Pope Francis speaks of this spiritual worldliness in his apostolic exhortation *Evangelii Gaudium*:

> Spiritual worldliness, which hides behind the appearance of piety and even love for the Church, consists in seeking not the Lord's glory but human glory and personal well-being. It is what the Lord reprimanded the Pharisees for: "How can you believe, who receive glory from one another and do not seek the glory that comes from the only God?" (Jn 5:44). It is a subtle way of seeking one's "own interests, not those of Jesus Christ" (Phil 2:21). It takes on many forms, depending on the kinds of persons and groups into which it seeps. Since it is based on carefully cultivated appearances, it is not always linked to outward sin; from without, everything appears as it should be. But if it were to seep into the Church, "it would be infinitely more disastrous than any other worldliness which is simply moral."[4]

Jesus desires us to experience the joy of poverty rather than the elusive sumptuousness of lavish and expensive living. I have previously addressed simplicity of life; but it is good to remember that the danger of things or lifestyle—even a possessiveness of our time, which is not our own in the first place—can get in the way of our service to God's people. Poverty of time is part of our death-to-self as a parish priest. The life of any adult is very busy. For instance, most parents work and then go to extracurricular events (sports, ballet, school activities) without any free time for themselves. The "new normal" for those of you who have gone directly from high school to college to major seminary is to realize that our lives of service as "fathers" will, likewise, take on a "busy-ness" about the Lord's affairs. Embrace poverty of time as a way of life—the days of two hours on PlayStation are over; of a movie every night are over; of being able to be free and spontaneous on a whim are over. They are not over because you are a seminarian or a priest but because you are an adult. Please learn to accept this as your "new normal." If you need to whine about it (and we all certainly do at times), talk to our Lord about it in prayer, with your spiritual director, and with your best friend; but do not wear it on your sleeve, and please do not burden the faithful with "how busy Father is."

I would also like to say a word about the so-called sacredness of our day off. Pope Francis writes about "priests who are obsessed with protecting their free time."

> This is frequently due to the fact that people feel an overbearing need to guard their personal freedom, as though the task of evangelization was a dangerous poison rather than a joyful response to God's love which summons us to mission and makes us fulfilled and productive. Some resist giving themselves over completely to mission and thus end up in a state of paralysis and acedia.
>
> The problem is not always an excess of activity, but rather activity undertaken badly, without adequate motivation, without a spirituality which would permeate it and make

it pleasurable. As a result, work becomes more tiring than necessary, even leading at times to illness. Far from a content and happy tiredness, this is a tense, burdensome, dissatisfying and, in the end, unbearable fatigue.[5]

We certainly need to take some time off on a weekly basis to find balance and rest in our life as seminarians and priests but not more than one day. Too often, the day off becomes a "sacred cow" or an idol that obscures our call "to serve and not be served." Talk with your pastor about his guidelines and expectations regarding your day off. Uncommunicated expectations by either of you are a recipe for disappointment.

We have been reminded many times by Pope Francis to have on us the "smell of the sheep"—our hands were meant for chalices, yes, but calluses too (for example, participating in parish work days, assisting with Knights of Columbus fish fries, setting up Holy Week, picking up bathrooms on Saturday night)! Get your hands dirty serving the faithful. We are ordained to be the servant of all in imitation of Christ. Our identity *in persona Christi* does not put us over the faithful but orders us to their service. Hierarchy does not mean I am *higher* than them, but *hier*—from the Greek *hierus* (a holy ordering). Think of the *Mandatum* of Holy Thursday night when Christ took the form of a slave, giving us the example of washing the feet of those entrusted to His care. Pope Francis spoke at the Chrism Mass on Holy Thursday of how we are to live this sense of servitude and littleness:

> I do not think it is an exaggeration to say that priest is very little indeed: *the incomparable grandeur of the gift granted us for the ministry sets us among the least of men.* The priest is the poorest of men unless Jesus enriches him

by his poverty, the most useless of servants unless Jesus calls him his friend, the most ignorant of men unless Jesus patiently teaches him as he did Peter, the frailest of Christians unless the Good Shepherd strengthens him in the midst of the flock. No one is more "little" than a priest left to his own devices; and so our prayer of protection against every snare of the Evil One is the prayer of our Mother: I am a priest because he has regarded my littleness (cf. Lk 1:48). And in that littleness we find our joy.[6]

Being Christ, *in persona Christi*, demands us to be Christ at all times. Therefore, we must know Him, encounter Him in our prayer, in our *lectio divina*, and in our way of life. The teenagers of my parish used to wear bracelets with the letters WWJD (What would Jesus do?) on them. Do we, who are "professional" religious people, strive to ask ourselves this question in our daily lives? Right now, at the seminary? *Christ: The Ideal of the Priest*[7] is the title of a book by Blessed Columba Marmion that I am giving to all the newly ordained this year. Do we strive to allow Christ to be our ideal at all times? Do we know Christ Jesus in order to imitate Him? Again, "What would Jesus do?"

Do our lives have a sense of radical availability, self-sacrifice, and pastoral presence? These are the hallmarks of real masculine spirituality. Our truest meaning and fulfillment are found in pastoral ministry! Why is it that so many little boys want to be firemen? Because a fireman rushes into dark buildings engulfed with smoke to save people. This is the rescue mission we are on! Real men rush into the darkness to bring light. We are not afraid to go to an accident scene where there have been fatalities or to the hospital to comfort parents who have lost a small child or enter into the murkiness of families breaking apart to try and bring healing. We are on a rescue mission, and it is precisely here that the *puer aeternus* is conquered and our manhood is discovered. Manhood is not found in chopping down trees or running Tough Mudders (however good these activities might be). Our manhood is discovered and actualized in our pastoral ministry, in laying down our lives in imitation of Christ. As Pope Francis said on Holy Thursday, "unless you 'exit' from yourself, the oil grows rancid and the anointing cannot be fruitful. Going out from ourselves presupposes self-denial; it means poverty."[8] This kind of poverty of time and possessions draws us out of a self-referential vantage point and gives us the perspective of Christ.

Presumptuous

It is evident the Holy Father is not speaking of pre-sumptuousness in reference to taking the grace of God for granted, but as a behavior or an attitude that is boldly arrogant and offensive. Clericalism at its worst is thinking we are superior to everyone around us and that we do not owe anyone an explanation for our behaviors or actions. A perfect example of how not to be presumptuous in the parish is by practicing good communication with your pastor and parish staff. We are accountable to these good people who are our coworkers in the vineyard; do not be secretive. Let the staff know what you are doing: "I am in the Church praying my Holy Hour." "I am headed to the hospital for an anointing." "I am going over to the school." "I will be in the rectory working on my homily." "I am going to exercise and I will be back in an hour." (I still tell Minnie, my assistant, where

I am going and what I am doing whenever I am not in the office—we must work as a team with those around us). The point is, our life is one of availability, and the staff help make it possible for us to be out of the office. Simple communication goes a long way toward harmony and efficiency.

At the same time, make sure to spend time in the office so you are available to the people you work with and the people who simply walk in (especially if you are the priest on duty). Take appointments. Hold meetings and meet with people in your office; it is visible, and there are generally always others present. Even with the office door closed for privacy, there should be windows on the door for the sake of propriety and transparency. Seclusion and isolation are deadly! The opposite of transparency is seclusion and isolation in the rectory which can easily be misperceived as either being aloof or hiding something

If you communicate well with the staff, they will be your biggest advocates. You might have the attitude that, "Well, I am a priest, and they don't need to know what I'm doing." This kind of mindset expresses the presumptuous and boldly arrogant attitude Pope Francis is talking about. We are a family and are called to work together. Families who do not communicate well are dysfunctional—and how often this happens in rectories and parish offices. The members of the staff are not our personal servants, but our coworkers. Talk things through with your pastor. Turn to him for advice; ask him every once in a while how you are doing. Be humble enough to take correction even after seminary formation is long over. This is part of our ongoing formation and conversion to be evermore shepherds after the Heart of Christ.

It is also presumptuous to think you can miss events or simply show up late for scheduled liturgical celebrations ("They can't start without me!"). I hear of occasions when priests oversleep and miss required parish events, sending the sacristans and other priests of the parish scrambling at the last minute—this is simply not fair to anyone! The self-centered and self-referential seminarian or priest does not see the needs of others before his own. This is precisely why we take seriously our need to be at seminary events—as they say, "So the seminarian, so the priest!"

The seminarian or priest whose life is unctuous, sumptuous, and presumptuous is not experiencing the fullness of Gospel joy. The Lord wants each of us to experience His oil of gladness. Avoiding being self-referential is not the end in itself, but a pathway to being freer to live our lives joyfully in relationship with Jesus and the people to whom He sends us to serve. I am very proud of you, and I have great hope for our Church because I believe you will bring health and healing to our people as you live out your anointing with humility, joy, and radically in love for the whole Body of Christ. As Pope Francis said: "The Lord anointed us in Christ with the oil of gladness, and this anointing invites us to accept and appreciate this great gift: the gladness, the joy of being a priest. Priestly joy is a priceless treasure, not only for the priest himself but for the entire faithful people of God: that faithful people from which he is called to be anointed and which he, in turn, is sent to anoint."[9]

I wish to close with section forty-nine from *Evangelii Gaudium*, which I feel sums up Pope Francis's vision and which will keep us from becoming self-referential seminarians and priests:

Let us go forth, then, let us go forth to offer everyone the life of Jesus Christ. Here I repeat for the entire Church what I have often said to the priests and laity of Buenos Aires: I prefer a Church which is bruised, hurting and dirty because it has been out on the streets, rather than a Church which is unhealthy from being confined and from clinging to its own security. I do not want a Church concerned with being at the centre and which then ends by being caught up in a web of obsessions and procedures. If something should rightly disturb us and trouble our consciences, it is the fact that so many of our brothers and sisters are living without the strength, light and consolation born of friendship with Jesus Christ, without a community of faith to support them, without meaning and a goal in life. More than by fear of going astray, my hope is that we will be moved by the fear of remaining shut up within structures which give us a false sense of security, within rules which make us harsh judges, within habits which make us feel safe, while at our door people are starving and Jesus does not tire of saying to us: "Give them something to eat" (Mk 6:37).[10]

Brothers, let us go forth to our parishes this summer and even out to the peripheries anointed with the "oil of gladness" and give the hungering world something to eat—the joy of the Gospel!

NOTES

1.   Cardinal Jorge Mario Bergoglio, as found in www.catholicnewsa-gency.com/column/evangelii-gaudium-exhorting-a-self-referential-church-2753 (Catholic New Agency, 5 December 2013, article by Fr. Thomas Berg, *"Evangelii Gaudium*: Exhorting a Self-Referential Church" (accessed 5/7/19).

2.   Donald Cozzens, *The Changing Face of the Priesthood* (Collegeville, MN: Liturgical Press, 2000), 75.

3.   Francis, *Evangelii Gaudium* (2013), sec. 78.

4.   Ibid., sec. 93.

5.   Ibid., sec. 81–82.

6.   Francis, *Holy Chrism Mass* (17 April 2014), para. 2. Emphasis added.

7.   Columba Marmion, *Christ: The Ideal of the Priest* (San Francisco, CA: Ignatius Press, 2005).

8.   *Holy Chrism Mass*, para. 9.

9.   Ibid., para. 1.

10.   *Evangelii Gaudium*, sec. 49.

Serving Versus Being Served: Jekyll and Hyde

I want to begin tonight with the image of a book written by Robert Louis Stephenson in 1886, *The Strange Case of Dr. Jekyll and Mr. Hyde*. According to Wikipedia:

> The work is commonly associated with the rare mental condition often called "split personality," referred to in psychiatry as dissociative identity disorder, where within the same body there exists more than one distinct personality. In this case, there are two personalities within Dr. Jekyll, one apparently good and the other evil. The novella's impact is such that it has become a part of the language, with the very phrase "Jekyll and Hyde" coming to mean a person who is vastly different in moral character from one situation to the next.[1]

Jekyll and Hyde are who we want to avoid becoming in our pastoral ministry, especially in our transition from the seminary to ordination.

To go through formation and act one way for the sake of the formation team and then act in a contrary way after being ordained because no one can tell you what to do—this is clericalism at its worst. This is what Pope Francis referred to when he warned seminary formators about not creating "little monsters."[2] Tonight, I am going to present a few vignettes, painting in broad strokes, even caricatures, in order to make the point. Dr. Jekyll was a well-respected and mild-mannered gentleman; but after taking a potion, he was transformed into a dangerous monster that hurt others. We certainly do not want to have such a "split personality" in our own lives.

Let us talk about the dutiful and diligent, hardworking seminarian who becomes a seemingly lackluster and lazy priest who shows no initiative. I hear pastors say that their associate does what is mandatory (shows up for Mass) but does not know how to engage the parish family. What does it mean to show up to activities that are not mandatory? Taking a walk through the school; visiting children in faith formation class; chatting during coffee and donuts; attending a basketball or volleyball game; being in the office during office hours even when you do not have scheduled appointments; and going to various meetings of the Knights of Columbus, the Rite of Christian Initiation of Adults (RCIA), the Womens' Guild, and other organizations, even if ever so briefly. I wonder sometimes if we do not set you up for this confusion in the seminary when we make the distinction of mandatory and optional—which often translates as: "I do not have to show up." Learn as a priest and as a father to show up. Yes, it takes time; but it also brings joy. It is the "good weariness" and "fruitful and joyful exhaustion" that Pope Francis spoke of on Holy Thursday:

> This weariness in the midst of activity is a grace on which all priests can draw (cf. [*Evangelii Gaudium*], 279). And how beautiful it is! People love their priests, they want and

need their shepherds! The faithful never leave us without
something to do, unless we hide in our offices or go
out in our cars wearing sun glasses. There is a good and
healthy tiredness. It is the exhaustion of the priest who
wears the smell of the sheep . . . but also smiles the smile
of a father rejoicing in his children or grandchildren. It
has nothing to do with those who wear expensive cologne
and who look at others from afar and from above (cf.
ibid., 97). We are the friends of the Bridegroom: this is
our joy. If Jesus is shepherding the flock in our midst,
we cannot be shepherds who are glum, plaintive or,
even worse, bored. The smell of the sheep and the smile
of a father. . . . Weary, yes, but with the joy of those
who hear the Lord saying: "Come, O blessed of my
Father" (Mt 25:34).[3]

Or how about that same dutiful and diligent, hardworking seminarian who *seemingly* becomes lackluster and lazy
because he is busy always protecting himself. Pastors tell me,
"Do not send me a Carthusian; send me a servant." We live
in a very regimented and structured environment here in the
seminary with a proper time for everything. In the parish,
there is a proper time for nothing—what do I mean by that?
In the seminary, you always know when you are going to pray
your Office, pray your Holy Hour, have Mass, eat your meals,
make time for exercise, and spend time in fraternity. In the
parish, flexibility must become your middle name! One sick
call to the hospital, one family crisis in the office, one angry
parent who walks over from the school can disrupt your
whole schedule. Or will you say, "I'm sorry; that is my nap
time"—or exercise time, or prayer time, or even your day off.
Learn to be flexible. Make adjustments on the fly, and die to

self in that moment. It is not easy, but this is what a father does for his children. Ask parents how they do it. They must sacrifice their own desires and comforts for the good of their children. That being said, I deeply want you to be men of prayer—making time for daily Mass, Liturgy of the Hours, silent intimacy with the Lord—but know that it might be at a different time each day or you may need to make adjustments midstream, or even pray late at night to catch up (I cannot tell you how many times I have had late night Holy Hours and Hours of the Office a little behind the *veritas horarum*).

Similarly, your health is very important to me and to the Church, but if something in our schedule has to give, it is often daily exercise—how I would love to be able to do something physical every day, but it is not realistic. If I can exercise three or four days a week for thirty to forty-five minutes, then I am doing great. You will not have time to go to LA Fitness for an hour and a half every day as a priest—realize this now, and adjust your expectations. Your work week will be sixty to eighty hours. This job does not come with a forty-hour work week—it is our vocation.

While our friends work from nine to five, our work is a little more all-encompassing because this is also our family. Our friends work eight hours and then run carpool and soccer practice, clean the house, and do the cooking. We do not have to take kids to soccer, but sometimes we need to take a walk out to the sports field and see "our" children play. If you think of priesthood as work, the eighty-hour week will exhaust you. Remember, I am counting prayer and Liturgy as part of our "work day." This is who we are. I recently heard from an old man the cliché: "Do what you love, and you will never work a day in your life!" If we accept this is our life, then we can find the joy Pope Francis mentioned at the Chrism Mass. We are not always going to love every moment of every day, but Jesus Christ gives meaning to all we do; and "where there is love, sacrifice is easy."[4]

Another vignette I would like to share is about the simple seminarian who exists on very little money but becomes the worldly, extravagant priest who not only liberally spends his own money, but also that of the parish. He goes from having absolutely zero money to being given thirty thousand dollars, of which practically all is disposable income. How easy it is for this man to allow spending to get out of control—buying clothes (both secular and clerical) and the latest gizmos and gadgets, receiving a constant wave of mail-order boxes that show up at the rectory, overspending on the parish credit card, or submitting every receipt as though he is owed everything. People often want to give us money for our services, and my response is, "This is what I get paid for—I actually *do* get a salary as a priest." The truth is that we really do not need more of anything. People will often give it anyway, and so be generous in giving it back—tithe abundantly to various organizations, including your own parish and alma mater! As the great Monsignor Gerry Finnegan of the Diocese of Venice in Florida would say, "never, ever, ever accept money at a sick call." This is just what we do. We may get a gift at a wedding or Baptism in addition to the parish offering, but *never* when we have gone to a house or hospital to anoint someone. In those cases, I always say, just put it in the poor box the next time you are at Church. Remember *Canon* 282:

> Clerics are to follow a simple way of life and avoid anything which smacks of worldliness.

Goods which they receive on the occasion of the
exercise of an ecclesiastical office, and which are over
and above what is necessary for their worthy upkeep
and the fulfillment of all the duties of their state, they
may well wish to use for the good of the Church and for
charitable works. [5]

Let me paint another picture of the middle-of-the-road,
very healthy seminarian who leaves the seminary only to
become the arch-conservative liturgical throwback to the
sixteenth century. Who are you? How were you formed?
Why did I never see this attitude? Where did you come from?
And most importantly, is this what the people of God need
you to be? I must admit that from time to time, I get blown
away by this one—priests who act like they know better than
their bishops, pastors, and certainly the seminary in which
they were trained, and come out with guns blazing to change
how their parish does just about everything. Okay, I get the
zeal, but not the imprudence and arrogance. Listen, learn,
and grow into a member of the new family to which you are
being sent.

Or how about the docile, obedient seminarian who, after
ten years of ordination, refuses to move when asked by the
bishop. Really? How did he not realize this is exactly what
obedience entails—to serve the greatest need of our diocese
as discerned by our bishop even when it is inconvenient.

Or the unprincipled seminarian who says all the right
things regarding celibacy to the formation team only to later
find himself in trouble from acting out in parish ministry
with a needy divorcée, a handsome young woman *or* man,
a wealthy widow, or—absolutely God forbid   a minor!

Brothers, the grass is always greener. This area is where we usually "weary ourselves"[6] as Pope Francis lamented at the Chrism Mass:

> But this third kind of weariness is more "self-referential:" it is dissatisfaction with oneself, but not the dissatisfaction of someone who directly confronts himself and serenely acknowledges his sinfulness and his need for God's mercy, his help; such people ask for help and then move forward. Here we are speaking of a weariness associated with "wanting yet not wanting," having given up everything but continuing to yearn for the fleshpots of Egypt, toying with the illusion of being something different. I like to call this kind of weariness "flirting with spiritual worldliness."[7]

When we straddle the fence and flirt with spiritual worldliness, especially in reference to celibacy, we exhaust ourselves! Pope Francis just published the Message for the 52nd World Day of Prayer for Vocations in which he reminds us:

> Jesus says: "Everyone who has left home or brothers or sisters or father or mother or children or lands, for my name's sake, will receive a hundredfold, and inherit eternal life" (Mt 19:29). All of this is profoundly rooted in love. The Christian vocation is first and foremost a call to love, a love which attracts us and draws us out of ourselves, "decentering" us and triggering "an ongoing exodus out of the closed inward-looking self towards its liberation through self-giving, and thus towards authentic self-discovery and indeed the discovery of God" (Deus Caritas Est, 6).[8]

I am always drawn back to Luke 9:62: "Jesus said 'No one who sets a hand to the plow and looks to what was left behind is fit for the kingdom of God.'" And remember the great line that I previously shared from Monsignor Preston Moss from the Archdiocese of Nassau in the Bahamas: "Keep your hands to the plow, even when they are bleeding!"

And now to the really mundane and immature: the seminarian who cleans his room before inspection and never integrates the virtue behind it, only to be black-balled by the priests of his diocese who do not want that slob in their rectories.

Or one more, the eager beaver who is very conscientious with his work, but who also says "Yes" to everything outside of the parish. Someone once told their pastor, "but Monsignor Toups does this." I just want to make clear that the responsibilities of the rector of a major seminary are very different from those of an associate pastor—when I leave for a meeting or a talk, there are ten other priests on campus. If you leave the parish, there may be only one left holding the bag and building up resentments toward you. Do not misunderstand me; there is an appropriate time and place to get involved outside the parish for the occasional youth retreat or college campus talk, but only in dialogue with your pastor and never at the detriment of your primary community. Always be faithful to being present to your parish first.

Now is the time to learn how to be a parish priest. To learn how to prioritize and distinguish the greater good at any given time, to distinguish the difference between unstructured time and free time. In other words, if you have only the Sunday 8:00 a.m. Mass, you are not free the rest of the day to tailgate at the Jags game (except on *very* rare occasions).

We must all learn to be personally responsible for the parish in which we serve. *You* will be the administration, not the Seminary CFO, the Vice Rector, nor the Rector; take initiative when you see a problem. When the school alarm goes off in the middle of night, it is your problem. This is your home; this is your parish. If you see something that needs to be fixed, fix it. If you hear an alarm going off, report it. Do not be afraid of work, laying down your life, and sacrificing for your family—"conform your life to the mystery of the Lord's cross."[9]

Ultimately, poor Dr. Jekyll longs to be free of the nagging Mr. Hyde who continues to drain him and drag him down. Do not be your own worst enemy! Be free and find points of integration all throughout your seminary career. "*Understand* what you do, *imitate* what you celebrate, and *conform* your life to the mystery of the Lord's cross."[10]

St. John Paul II wrote:

> "[I]t is vital to educate future priests to have the virtue of penance, which the Church wisely nourishes in her celebrations and in the seasons of the liturgical year, and which finds its fullness in the sacrament of reconciliation. From it flow the sense of asceticism and interior discipline, a spirit of sacrifice and self-denial, the acceptance of hard work and of the cross. These are elements of the spiritual life which often prove to be particularly arduous for many candidates for the priesthood who have grown up in relatively comfortable and affluent circumstances and have been made less inclined and open to these very elements."[11]

As Pope Francis concluded his Chrism Mass homily, so do I tonight:

> Our discipleship itself is cleansed by Jesus, so that we can rightly feel "joyful," "fulfilled," "free of fear and guilt," and impelled to go out "even to the ends of the earth, to every periphery." In this way we can bring the good news to the most abandoned, knowing that "he is with us always, even to the end of the world." And please, let us ask for the grace to learn how to be weary, but weary in the best of ways![12]

NOTES

1. *Wikipedia*, s.v. "*Strange Case of Dr Jekyll and Mr Hyde*," last modified February 4, 2019, http://en.wikipedia.org/wiki/Strange_Case_of_Dr_ Jekyll_and_Mr_Hyde (accessed 5/6/19).

2. See https://www.americamagazine.org/content/all-things/ pope-warns-poorly-trained-priests-can-become-little-monsters.

3. Francis, *Holy Chrism Mass* (2 April 2015), para. 12.

4. A line from the popular USCCB vocational film, *Fishers of Men* (http://www.usccb.org/beliefs-and-teachings/vocations/priesthood/ fishers-of-men.cfm [accessed 5/7/19]).

5. *Code of Canon Law: Latin-English Edition: New English Translation (Codex Iuris Canonici [CIC])*, (Washington, DC: Canon Law Society of America, 1998), c. 282, secs. 1–2.

6. See Francis, *Evangelii Gaudium* (24 November 2013), sec. 277.

7. *Holy Chrism Mass*, para. 14.

8. Francis, "Message for the 52nd World Day of Prayer for Vocations" (26 April 2015), para. 3. http://w2.vatican.va/content/francesco/ en/messages/vocations/documents/papa-francesco_20150329_52- messaggio-giornata-mondiale-vocazioni.html (accessed 5/6/19).

9. U.S. Conference of Catholic Bishops, *Rites of Ordination of a Bishop, of Priests, and of Deacons* (Washington, DC: USCCB, 2003), 111.

10. Ibid.

11. John Paul II, *Pastores Dabo Vobis* (1992), sec. 48.

12. *Holy Chrism Mass*, para. 17.

A Priest's Prayer of Consecration to Mary[1]

O Holy and Immaculate Virgin Mary,
I consecrate to you the priesthood entrusted to me by your Divine Son,
Jesus the Great High Priest—I am all yours and all that I have I give
to you.
Be my tender and loving Mother and remind me daily that I am a
beloved son of God the Father.
May your docile "yes" to the invitation of the Holy Spirit inspire me to
be a humble servant of your Eucharistic Son as He once again becomes
incarnate in my hands.
Mary, you are the model of the Church, the Bride of Christ, help me to
live a life worthy of my noble calling to be a chaste-spouse and spiritual-
father to the Church.
Reveal the beauty of your face in order that I may be comforted in my
frustrations; may I be purified and dwell within by your Immaculate
Heart in union with the Sacred Heart of Jesus.
St. Joseph the Worker, teach me to be the man that the Father wants me
to be—laying down my life and sacrificing for my Bride in the same way
you cared for the Holy Family.
O Jesus, Divine Physician and Good Shepherd, heal me that I might
heal, lead me that I might lead all people into the Love of the Heart
of the Trinity—where You live and reign with the Father and the Holy
Spirit, One God forever and ever.
Amen.

NOTES

1.   David L. Toups, *Reclaiming Our Priestly Character* (Omaha: The Institute for Priestly Formation, 2008, revised edition 2010), 221-222.

CPSIA information can be obtained
at www.ICGtesting.com
Printed in the USA
FSHW012350060919